British Library Cataloguing-in-publication data
A catalogue record for this book is available from the British Library

Published by Izzy Publishing
Happy Endings
P.O. Box 888
Bromley, Kent BR1 9EP

ISBN 0-9552476-2-4
ISBN 978-0-9552476-2-0

www.izzypublishing.co.uk
mcrowcroft@aol.com

First Edition 2008

Printed and bound by Lightning Source

Illustrations by Maria Alexander

Angel Adventures

*Guided meditations that take
you on a journey to meet your angels*

written and illustrated by

Maria Alexander

This book is dedicated to my family:
my mother Kate Crowcroft who has been so supportive to me,
my wonderful sisters Anna Crystal and Lis Moon,
and her husband, Paul.
Lastly, my father Peter Crowcroft who taught me how to write
as well as the importance of following your vision.

This book is also dedicated to all the 'earth angels'
who have helped me and to all who are on the path
of self-improvement and discovery.

Many thanks to Lis Spiro for her help with editing and corrections
and also to Suzie at Commercial Campaigns
for her wonderful layout and design.

Thanks also to the wonderful mysterious love, light and joy that is
available to all of us from the creator and the angels.

Chapters & Illustrations

Introduction
How to use this Book

Welcome to Angel Adventures! In this book you will be taken to the Land of the Angels where you will meet various Angels - a different one in each chapter. The cards will lead you intuitively to which Angel is the right one for you to talk to at the moment.

In the 'Beginning Your Journey' part of the book you will be taken to the Land of the Angels and guided to a lovely place just outside the Angel's Palace where, one by one, you will meet various Angels who will talk to you about their own particular subject and often take you on an adventure. It might be something as simple as meeting someone you still have issues with or it might be travelling to the outer levels of the universe. The adventures are designed to bring your imagination into the learning and healing process. Many believe our imagination can be a link into the higher realms.

If you just have the book:

1. Read the chapter titled: 'Beginning your journey.'
2. Close the book and then open at random to see what chapter you have opened to. Read that Angel Adventure as that is the one that is best for you at the moment.
3. You can repeat this process several times.

If you buy the Angel Adventure cards that accompany the book:

1. Read the Chapter titled 'Beginning Your Journey'.
2. Place the cards face down and then think of a question or a problem you have. You may even just want to ask for guidance. Then see which card you are intuitively attracted to. Turn this card over.
3. You can then find the chapter relating to that card and read the adventure.
4. You may like to meditate on the card that you chose. What meaning could this quality have in your life? Is there anything you have learned?

How often you travel to the Land of the Angels is up to you. You can visit every day or wait until you have a particular question. In using this book you might want to focus on one chapter a week and write down the chapter title somewhere that you will see it every day. Or you could work on one you feel you need for longer. So relax, stay light and have fun seeing what images happen for you as you meet with the Angels in this book. Learn their secrets and see if you can bring some of them back to earth. Let your intuition guide you. There is no right or wrong.

Remember the Angels are aware of you and your journey with all your struggles. They are always near to give loving help and support.

Good luck.

Beginning your Journey

It is night and you are lying in your bed. Looking through the window you see moonlight stream in and the stars twinkling in the dark sky. You turn away into your pillow and are lost in dreams of adventure when suddenly you hear a tapping on your window. Sleepily you sit up and look through your window to see a young Angel. She is about the size of a teenager and dressed all in white. Pale blond curls stream in the wind and blue eyes sparkle mischievously.

You notice that not only is she wearing white but also she is engulfed in a white light. She has wings, which are moving slowly to keep her stationary, and she seems to glow from within. In fact, she is almost transparent. Quickly you get out of bed and your bare feet touch the floor. As you move to the window it magically opens even before you touch it.

"Come on" she says, "I want to take you somewhere."

"Who are you and where are we going?" You ask.

"We are going to the world of the Angels. It is time for you to learn more and to develop spiritually. I am Astra. I am to lead you there. They are all waiting. Come, take my hand. Don't be afraid."

Strangely her words don't startle you and in fact a thrill of excitement and anticipation begins within you. For you feel that mysteries and magic may be unfolding for you.

As you take her hand she guides you onto the window ledge and then, with her leading the way you are pulled up into the air! You don't feel afraid as you feel yourself gently floating upwards towards the night sky. Looking down you see your home and the street you live in all becoming smaller.

Now Astra is moving faster and pulling you along. A cool wind is on your face from the speed as you fly over your town, moving higher, over your country, over forests and lakes, over islands and oceans, over the stars and past the moon...and then you are travelling out into the universe...still in your night clothes.

A shooting star passes you by so close that you can feel the heat of its golden sparks. For what seems like an age you travel through space. You pass the Milky Way and looking back you can see Earth.

"There it is!" calls Astra, against the wind and ahead you can see a small planet surrounded by a gold, violet and pink haze. As you approach you can see distinct forms of land and water, very different from the ones on earth. You are moving too fast to take in everything but suddenly you see a structure: something between a palace and a temple. A magnificent edifice which appears to be made out of a substance similar to quartz crystal. Yet this crystal has a warm golden glow and a rainbow of other colours visible inside the stone. Around the building you see beautiful Angels dressed in different coloured robes flying in and out of this structure.

"We are expected at the Palace of the Angels." She tells you and you find her guiding you towards the palace.

The sun is shining and you sense that this is an incredibly happy place. Beautiful gardens are visible with strange plants and flowers you have never seen before and near the palace lies a large body of silken water. Music is coming from somewhere with an enchanting voice singing something so piercingly lovely you almost want to cry. The colours are more vibrant here and the scent of flowers as you descend it delights your senses.

You alight with Astra on the cool crystal stone steps in front of an ornate front door.

"It won't take so long for you to arrive here next time." Astra tells you. "With just a thought you can be here."

The door opens immediately and a lovely Angel in purple robes smiles at you. She has an aura of being very wise and as you look in her eyes you feel such love there that you feel totally relaxed and protected.

"Welcome. We have been expecting you. We rejoice that you have come to learn our ways and hope that you will enjoy the time we spend together. My name is Hera."

She leads you inside. You may be wondering why you are here. You may or may not know that Angels can hear your thought and prayers. The Creator knows that you seek more wisdom and balance in your life. You seek to find different ways in which to approach situations you find difficult. Hopefully, you can gain insight into your own behaviour and choices here and let go of some negativity.

"May I first say that many of us here have been watching you and we love you dearly. We see how hard you try and we feel for your set backs, although your path has not been easy you have learned and grown so much. Just know that help and love are available here any time you need them." She embraces you lovingly. You feel her love as gentle heart tingling warmth that reminds you of when you were a child. You linger in that loving embrace for a few moments as a bird sings outside the window.

"You will be visited by 14 other Angels." Hera tells you. "Each one will take you on a guided adventure to experience an aspect of our world or to learn something about yourself. There is much beauty and harmony here. Relax and progress at your own pace. Sometimes wisdom takes a lifetime to achieve. Be at peace."

Now Astra will lead you, find you some robes to wear and then take you to the grounds where you will be brought refreshment and can relax. When you are ready the first Angel will visit you. Her message will be the one most needed at the moment. I will also visit you at some time to discuss wisdom. Now go and peace be with you. Just stay there and enjoy the peace and Astra will be back to fetch you when it is time."

You step into a small room that contains a chair and a window that looks out onto the garden. The sun is starting to descend and it is that magical time of sunset. You find on the chair robes in your favourite colour. You change into them and then sit in the chair and watch the light dance on the trees outside the window. You feel very peaceful.

Once you have changed Astra finds you and leads you back outside the temple and down the marble steps to the grounds around the Palace. The lawns are set out around a fountain that you have already noticed with beds and pergolas of exotic flowers. The scents are intoxicating and relaxing at the same time. You see a comfortable chair next to a small table.

"This is the Garden of Contemplation. As you wait here a different Angel will collect you and teach you about different subjects. You will travel to different places and have interesting adventures." She tells you. You feel in the mood for an adventure but first you feel that you would like to sit in the comfortable chair by the small table nearby, where you now notice there is something pleasant to drink. "I will leave you now." Astra tells you. "But you won't be alone for long. Farewell."

You thank her, have a sip of the drink and then lie back and relax.

Inner Peace
The Angel of Divine Light

Sitting in the Garden of Contemplation you notice a misty blue and silver light forming nearby. The light grows and grows until you see it has formed into an Angel wearing flowing iridescent robes of soft rose. Silk flaxen hair falls around her shoulders. An aura of peace and tranquillity surrounds her and you feel immediately at ease.

"Greetings." She says to you. "I am the Angel of Divine Light. We have watched you and seen that you have in your life what is known as 'stress' in your world. I am here to guide you to inner peace and balance. Would that be acceptable to you?"

It sounds as if it something you need so you smile and tell her yes.

"Good. First let us talk about the value of inner peace." She says. "Inner peace heals. Inner peace is a connection to your spiritual self. You achieve it through physical relaxation in the body, emotional calm, and mental focus on higher ideals and qualities. If you wish to go upward, to experience and live in higher levels of energy, inner peace is the doorway."

Inner peace is a connection to your deeper self, and it will assist you in letting go of fear. Fear is a lower energy, a vibration of less light, and can be changed by love. One of the goals of having inner peace is healing fear.

You feel you want to speak out and ask questions and, although shy, you do speak your mind.

"How can I have inner peace when my life isn't as I want it to be?" You ask. She smiles.

"One of the greatest ways to experience inner peace is to practise acceptance. This with forgiveness and love can turn most situations around. Acceptance is just living in the now of what is - not the past or the future. Not guilt or hope or fear. It is accepting people as they are and not expecting them to change. If you want to help them and they change, then that is good but it's different. That is up to them.

"But I can't feel peaceful because I'm so tense!" You tell her.

She moves closer and you are fascinated by the play of light around her.

"What you call tension of the muscles begins in the mind with worry. If you have problems then pray for guidance and let go of the worry. It only affects the body adversely. If you stay balanced and calm then your thoughts will be clearer and you can make better decisions."
She closes her eyes and almost seems to be communicating with another world.

"What ruins inner peace? What are some things we need to give up? Fear, anger, worry, sadness, guilt, longing, desire, emotional pain and hate are some of the emotional states we need to let go of before we can start to feel inner peace.

Minds are amazing things. They chatter constantly and create opinions, dramas and judgements about who we are. But often they are just ideas - empty as clouds. "

"A lot of the time I'm judging myself" You say, and the Angel of Divine Light nods.

"Our minds can sometimes be our own judge and jury. But we are not just our minds. When you were a baby before your mind was 'trained' you were pure consciousness, full of love and wonder and happy to be in the world. As you grew and explored your world this continued until you started thinking, judging and worrying over what we and other people thought and did. You learned to feel bad about yourself: insecure and unworthy. You learned to fear the future. What would happen if you stopped the chatter in your mind and just existed from one moment to another not anticipating, just experiencing?"

You think about this for a moment before answering her. "I would probably be able to relax a bit more." You admit. The Angel nods and smiles.

"Good. We will go on several journeys but I also want to show you some techniques for calming the mind. "

"But why are Angels so peaceful? You ask her."

She is silent for a few moment and then answers.

"Our inner peace comes from our connection with the divine energy that flows through us. It brings to us an acceptance of how things are and the belief that we are all being lovingly guided to our higher good - no matter how it may appear on the surface. The Angels peace also manifests from a deep sense of love and compassion towards each person in the world."

Then she opens her eyes and continues.

"A good technique to calm the mind is to meditate upon things that you love. This could be a piece of music, nature, your children or anything that brings you joy. Put aside time to meditate, especially if you are going through a difficult time. At other times see a peaceful scene in your mind. Your thoughts can be gently guided into peaceful waters. Also you can think of the word 'peace' and say this word to yourself over and over as you go through your day then you will find your attitude to life becoming more peaceful."

She pauses for a moment.

"Now we will go on a journey. Come with me. Some say life is a river and one merely needs to flow with it. You can experience this now..." She takes your hand and suddenly you find yourself in another dimension: the dimension of spirit. Your body is pure energy and light.

You are aware of the Angel holding your hand but you feel your spirit flying down from the higher realms of light into the earth plane again. You land on the earth and see someone you recognise. It is you in your former earth life. There you are worrying about some situation or problem and how it will be resolved. You remember that everything happened for a reason and most things were resolved. But the eternal dimensions where you reside now are so lovely that you with you wish you could have remembered them when you were on the earth.

"As you move closer to your earth self you can send images of the future and allow yourself to release the fears and worries as you are surrounded with a loving golden light. All is well. You are protected and loved. " She tells you.

Now you find yourself flying high above the land of the Angels. You see the sun shining on fields, meadows and forests of green. Between the meadows and forests a startling thread of blue shows itself as a river, winding its way through the countryside to the sea.

"This is the sea of Tranquillity." The Angel of Divine Energy says as she guides you down...down...down towards this water.

"Are we going swimming?" You joke.

She laughs. "You'll see." She tells you.

You slowly alight on the water and feel your feet touch the surface. As they do your body becomes a different substance and you feel yourself turning into liquid. It is very pleasant feeling. The Angel releases you and your pour into the water which is now the same element as yourself. You can breathe easily and as you move downstream, you become aware of the river's slow, gentle progress and the weight of the water. You are part of the river, gently flowing and ebbing with the current.

Drifting to the distant bank where wild flowers grow, you lazily watch the sunlight as it dances through the trees on the water creating

PEACE

patterns of golden light. Lush trees grow on the riverbanks...willow trees, their branches swaying gently in the soft breezes as you drift by. Feel the gentle flow of water. The river moves gently and you are part of it. You sense energy everywhere: in the plants at the bottom of the river and in the fish swimming,

Hummingbirds and colourful butterflies play in the flowers and trees, creating songs of joy at being alive. You savour all of this as you drift down this timeless river...you can't see clearly where you are going as there are many turns in the river up ahead. But you feel so peaceful...so safe and relaxed as you let the water pull you gently along with it. You know you can flow with every event in your life...it is all part of your river.

After a few miles of this gentle travelling you have forgotten who you are and what your name is. Then you feel a hand take yours and raise you up out of the water. Almost immediately you return to your usual form but in a daze you stare at the Angel.

"Now you see that nature has her own rhythms and when we align ourselves with them we experience peace." She says.

Still in a daze you notice that you are dry and she is taking you up higher into the sky. You are going into the night where a few moments ago you were in the daylight and as you break out of the atmosphere surrounding the planet you find yourself in the outer universe again. But somehow this feels different.

"Now I will show you why Angels are so peaceful." The angel says as she guides you up into the sky and into the universe where planets and stars twinkle. From here you can sense a gentle energy which feels like love and there is a shimmer of light falling like rain." The Angel closes her eyes and puts her head back in bliss.

"This is Divine Energy. It is the nectar of all Angels and gives us our power. It is God's love raining down on all things and us. Close your eyes. Let it flow through you."

You close your eyes. You can sense a wonderful energy that you can't describe. Your body relaxes and opens to this energy that feels so good. It feels like all the best feelings you have ever known. It feels as if your soul is suspended in a timeless place of beauty and wonder. You want to stay there forever. It feels like being in love. This love flows through you in waves of happiness. You feel loved. You feel accepted. You feel safe.

Eventually you open your eyes and see the Angel smiling at you. She nods and you know that no words are necessary. You have found inner peace. Your body is completely relaxed and feels good. Your mind is calm and you feel one with the universe.

"It is time to return to the Garden of Contemplation." She tells you.

Your first thought is that you don't want to leave. But part of you knows somehow that there is a time for everything and a gentle voice whispers that you can return to this place at any time.

When you return to the garden she hands you a piece of paper upon which is written an affirmation.

"Try to read this out loud or to yourself every day." She says as she smiles and disappears.

Affirmation:

Let me today experience peace. It is within that I find the infinite peace...the light and the truth that is love.

Truth
The Angel of Radiant Light

Sitting in the Garden of Contemplation you muse on your recent experiences in the world of the Angels. Then you notice a small bright light hovering near you. On closer inspection you discover that it is a candle suspended in mid air. Just as you are wondering at this, a form appears around the candle – an Angel with long dark hair, dressed in white robes.

She holds the candle high and says to you "I am the Angel of Radiant Light. Behold the light of truth. This is what I am here to discuss with you."

You sense purity and passion in the Angel. Then you realise she is speaking.

"Throughout the ages the philosophers and religious people have tried to define truth as they see it. Many have touched on answers that have rung true for millions. To discover a great truth - whether it is the law of gravity or a realization of a truth in you, can be very powerful. Every person has their own truth. We are each responsible for our own truth: our universe and how we perceive it. That is why in some ways truth is relative as we are ever changing and our perceptions change as well: who we are, what we want, what our role in the cosmos is, our morals and visions. Be true to yourself and what your intuition tells you. Come, we will go on a journey into the Cave of Secrets."

Taking you by the hand she leads you up into the air. You travel for what seems like hours but it is in fact only a few moments. Then you see ahead a mountain range. The peaks are in the clouds where white snow glistens with blue sparkles. Looking at the base of the mountain you see jagged inlets and caves.

"These are the Mountains of Wisdom." She tells you, the candle lighting the way like a star in the night. "The mountain contains many caves. We will visit one in particular."

Without warning she swoops you downwards towards the caves and you are afraid you are going to lose her grasp and fall. Looking below you see it is a long way down. Cold air rushes in your face and your hair

TRUTH

blows out behind you. You are aware of the cold and know that although you wear light robes you don't feel cold in the rest of your body.

"Hold on!" The Angel calls as she drops altitude very fast. You catch your breath. Then suddenly, your feet land on a rocky base dusted with a light covering of snow. Looking up you notice you are outside the entrance to a cave. Glancing up higher the mountain looms above you and the wind dislodges a small amount of snow which falls on your nose. The Angel notices this.

"Quickly." She says and you feel there is a no nonsense air about her.

"In the cave."

"What is this place?" you ask.

"The Cave of Secrets?" She muses. "It's a storehouse really. Every secret that a human keeps to themselves...good or bad is sent here. Look."
Saying this she lifts the candle high and you see a cave that seems a storeroom of boxes. Some are gold and some are tied with coloured ribbons. You pick up a small one and look at the contents. It reads: 'Secrets hidden from July 16, 1985.'

"What I brought you here to see is when I shine this candle on the secrets they disappear." The Angel tells you." She raises the candle high and the light from the flame fills the room.

The contents of the boxes turn to golden sand and then disappear.

"Come. It is time to move on." She tells you. Taking your hand you feel a wind blow around your hair and when you open your eyes you find you are on the earth again in an apartment. A couple are arguing. "What is going on?"

The Angel of Radiant Light shrugs. "Secrets. They have both been lying to each other. They've been withholding the truth and now one has discovered this and is it more upsetting than if they had learned the truth at the beginning."

You think about this. "Surely it depends what the truth is. If one of them is cheating them perhaps the other doesn't want to know."

"But they will find out at some point. Then they have the truth and the deception or omission of the lie to contend with. But they are venting their feelings and being honest now. This could help them to clear the cobwebs and have a better understanding of each other. Let's move on."

You are beginning to realize that the Angel of Truth likes to travel very quickly from one place to another and you aren't sure you can keep up. For a moment or two you wonder where you are going before everything turns pitch black.

Then you realise that you are in a field at sunrise on a winter morning. It is dark but not cold. Several people are here and behind them are standing stones, illuminated by the first rays of sunlight.

"These people are experimenting with energy." She tells you. "Do you see the energy field around their body?" She asks. Their words and thoughts become vibrations in the air that affect the people they are thinking or speaking about. They can see their effects of the cause of their thoughts and words.

Looking closely you see that they are indeed fields of energy around each person's body. Bands of colour are visible in the energy field. Each person's colours are different.

"These are aura's. The colours change depending on the person's mood and other factors."

The Angel indicates another couple on the outskirts of the group.

"Now watch these two. They are experimenting with the truth. They speak their own truth in a loving way to each other. Their auras change colour and become purer. They are obviously happier."

"We are always engaging in an energy transfer with other people. Sometimes we are taking energy sometimes we are giving it. We can actually help towards healing people if we send them good energy. As you live more in truth with yourself and others you will notice a change, a shift in the vibration of your energy. Being honest is important for growth".

"Being truthful begins with yourself." She tells you. "Now, close your eyes." She tells you and you do so. "Think of ways you have not been truthful with yourself."

Thinking carefully you realise that there are things crying out in you. Thoughts present themselves to you that would improve your life. You realise that you have not been listening to your deepest needs.

You realize the Angel is speaking. "Think of your better qualities and some you need to improve. Are you too hard on yourself? Could you be kinder to yourself? If you are harsh with yourself then you may be harsh with others. Sometimes our relationships can be a reflection of our relationship with ourselves. Close your eyes again." She tells you and you close your eyes.

"Now see someone you have not been truthful with. We are working through some of our illusions about what is true. Is it really another person we hate or despise or something in ourselves we are not able to forgive. When we forgive ourselves what will our truth be then? The more we heal inside then the more we are in touch with our deepest truth which is more to do with Joy and Love. You are also thinking of some ways you want to speak to someone and some ways you have not been honest with yourself and others.

Let me leave you with this thought." She says to you. "To thine own self be true as long as you don't hurt others. Now see the next step you need to take to put one of those things into action." She tells you. The next steps seems obvious to you.

"Good. Now open your eyes."

As she leaves she gives you a piece of paper with an affirmation on it:

Affirmation:

I speak my own truth, as I perceive it, yet with sensitivity for others. I know being honest allows others to be the same and builds trust and communication.

Forgiveness
The Angel of Harmony

You are visiting in the Garden of Contemplation when suddenly the season seems to change before your eyes. Whereas on your last visit it was summer now it is autumn. Instead of being by the bench you find yourself standing in a wood by a lake. The trees are wearing golden colours touched by flaming red and deep ochre. They fall gently onto the surface of the lake and glide along the water. They fall into your hand - crisp and perfect in their beauty. Walking to the lakeside you dip your fingers in the water. You hear the lapping of the water against the muddy banks and somewhere you hear music...so sweet and clear. You smell wood smoke and the promise of winter - the rich earth welcoming the leaves to her. Now the leaves are falling faster as a gentle wind lifts them off the trees. There is a special smell in the crisp air that signals the coming of winter. You become aware, in a pleasant way, that you are not alone. You sense an Angel standing next to you.

"I hope I didn't startle you! Dear me, no that would never do! I'm the Angel of Harmony, dear and I've been asked to talk to you about forgiveness. Why don't we walk along that path over there." She points to a path you have not noticed before. You feel her generous spirit, a motherly warm laughter and affection emanating from the Angel. It is relaxing.

"I do hope you aren't too cold! It's just my favourite time of the year and it's lovely to have your surroundings as you would like them, don't you think?" She asks you, as she rambles in a pleasant way.

You imagine what it would be like to change the weather as it suited you. "I like autumn too." You tell her as you both start along the path. She reminds you of a favourite aunt who is slightly confused.

"I'm so glad. What am I here for? Oh forgiveness...that's right. You know they are all related these lessons. Sometimes to accept a situation you need to forgive someone. Even yourself. Forgiveness can be considered the pathway to some of the higher feelings. As you progress on the spiritual path you will be tested with your level of ability to forgive. Forgiveness is not complete until you have come the other side of it and want to see them as happy. You've met the Angel of Truth I believe."

You nod. "She's a bit intense."

The Angel of Harmony nods and laughs in a very motherly way.

"Yes. The poor dear takes it all a bit seriously. But she means well and is just very passionate about her subject. You see with me I know people are not always ready to forgive. In fact one person took three hundreds years and six lifetimes to forgive someone...but that's another story... So all I can do is pave the way for when they are. But the Angel of Truth well she wants everyone to be truthful all the time. I'm afraid she wants a perfect world and we just aren't there yet. Oh! Here we are!"

You find yourself outside an unusual door. It is very ornately carved and you are fascinated and long to know what is inside the room. As you turn the handle you find yourself in a room with all your favourite type of furniture. It is a peaceful room. All the colours are peaceful. All around are comfortable familiar objects - a soft chair is pulled up to a warm fire outside the diamond paned windows.

You feel safe and cosy in the room lined with shelves of much loved books and peppered by antiques and treasured items. A warm fire crackles in the fireplace.

"Now that's much better. This is a nice place for us to talk." She says in delight holding her hands against the warmth of the fire. "Why don't you put on that sweater?"

On a table you find a bulky sweater and a mug of something warm and pleasant. You wrap the sweater around you and settle back in the big armchair by the fire with the hot drink in a big mug on the table next to you. You feel so relaxed you close your eyes.

"Oh dear...no we can't get comfortable yet! We have a few places to visit." The Angel tells you. "First I want to show you what lack of forgiveness can do in the extreme."

Before you can say anything the room and the mug are gone. You are aware of flying with her in a rush through the autumn winds but soon you find yourself on the earth plane on a city street at night. It is winter and the air seems cold.

"That is why I wanted you to wear the sweater!" She tells you. "It gets a bit nippy here in winter."

In front of you, walking with a stick, an elderly man is talking to himself as he makes his way past the houses.

"Sadly that man is full of anger and rage." The Angel tells you. She sighs with regret. "He has isolated himself from his family and everyone

FORGIVENESS

else because of real or imagined slights. No one wants to come near him because of the way he acts and he lives in self righteous solitude."

"How sad. " You say.

"Indeed." She agrees. "On a physical level it has affected him deeply. He has ground his teeth from anger for so long that he has very bad dental problems. His stomach has been in knots for so long with rage that he has created ulcers and the rigidity in his attitude and body affects his muscles causing more discomfort. The poor man is in physical as well as mental pain. He holds some hurts very deeply."

"If he had forgiven people would it have helped him physically?" You ask.

"Oh." The Angel explains. "I'm not saying he would be physically perfect but he would not have all those emotions tearing him to pieces."

You look back at the man talking to himself bitterly about someone he feels has wronged him you wish that he had been able to let go of the hurt and forgive.

"You know they say," says the Angel "Everyone is open and loving or expressing their past hurt. But only those with awareness can hear this call."

"But it's not easy to forgive." You remind her, thinking of some of your own experiences.

"Oh but apart from every other argument it simply feels good to forgive." She bubbles "Just as love feels better than a negative emotion, so too forgiveness feels better than holding on to emotional pain inside where it might fester for years if unchecked. That's why forgiveness is a selfish act. You are the main one who benefits. Just as if you don't you are the main one who suffers. There is always a choice. The other person could be alive or dead...affected or unaffected by your decision. Yet you will have made a shift in the vibration of all the energy in the world as well as your own vibrational level." She giggles. "You know laughter, warmth and friendship are good for the health and the heart." Her warmth is infectious and you find yourself laughing and smiling when you look at her.

"Come." The Angel says, "Let me take you somewhere else." Now I will show you a family who will not forgive and let go of some slights that happened before they were born."

You are at a funeral. A man and three women stand at the graveside wearing black.

"Their father was physically abusive and they all bear the internal scars and are reacting to the world out of that pain." The Angel tells you. " He treated them shamelessly. However he knew no better as he himself was beaten by his father until he was older and could start fighting back."

"In an abusive relationship sometimes understanding can be a first step to forgiveness - again it isn't condoning abuse or staying in it but it is looking past the behaviour to the pain, fear and confusion that lies underneath. Abusers are usually victims themselves."

"How are they reacting to that?"

"One of the women tries to be a perfectionist...the other is terrified of people. The man ruins every relationship he is in, afraid that he will end up like his father and the other travels constantly...trying to run away."

"Will they ever change?" You ask her.

"They can arrive at an awareness in time. Like all parts of our lives their experience is full of lessons for them."

As you watch the siblings you think about her words and wonder how long it will take them to heal. There is a long pause. Then she speaks again. " Well, let us return to our room in the forest."

With a whoosh you are back in the room in the forest. It is night time outside and rain and leaves from the branches of the trees tap gently on the window. It takes you a few moments to catch your breath and get your bearings. Then you realize that you and the Angel are not alone in the room.

Light from a glowing fire throws golden colour across the ceiling and you notice that two chairs are in the middle of the room. In one chair is someone you know. It is someone you have feelings of anger for. It is deep and won't be budged.

You sit in the chair and start talking to them. You feel embarrassed at first but then you sit and ask the person something you have never asked them before. Waiting you hope to hear a reply and learn something. Then they speak. As they speak you see their sadness and hurt. You become aware that the Angel is standing behind you. She whispers in your ear.

"You may or you may not feel you are ready to forgive them." The Angel tells you. "If you are not ready then at least you have more awareness of yourself and why you are not ready to let go of your anger. One useful technique in forgiveness is seeing the person as a child. You would have a hard time holding onto your resentment against a child of three or five especially if it was your child. There is nothing you could not forgive because it is your family."

You glance at the Angel and then look again at the chair opposite you and see that the person you were talking to has become a child of about 3 years old. They are sitting there looking lost and confused. Unbidden you feel a swelling of love and compassion for this child and you know that somehow it is a relative of yours. Holding out your arms to the child you allow it to climb into your lap and cry on your shoulder. Saying soothing words you stroke its hair and as you do your anger melts and a new, deeper understanding unfolds within you.

"Now it is time to return to the Garden of Contemplation." She tells you and you feel a rush of autumn air and find that you are both flying through the skies. The Garden looks different as you arrive there. The leaves have fallen from the trees and are strewn on the ground near the bench.

"I know I'm going to get angry again." You tell her. "What can I do?"

"To heal anger it is good to create an alter - somewhere you can meditate or pray every day. Bring to mind the person you are having difficulty with and start to visualise their happiness. See them starting to smile and feel joyful. If you know something that would make them happy - see them receiving it. Then you know you are free."

When you are near the bench she hands you a scrap of paper.

"If there is someone you are angry with say this on a regular basis then if you see them again they will feel the shift in your energy as you will have released your anger."

Affirmation:

I forgive myself and I forgive you, there is only forgiveness between us.
I love myself and I love you - there is only love between us.

You turn to thank her but she is gone and only a few autumn leaves fall at your feet.

Patience
The Angel of Eternity

The next Angel arrives in a soft yellow glow. As she becomes clearer to you amongst the yellow glow you see she is wearing a dress of gold and yellow and carries a spherical light which from which emanates various colours.

"Hello." She smiles. "I am here to talk to you about patience. We notice that in your world you are always rushing to be somewhere else. You always seem impatient for things to happen quicker, if not physically then mentally. You are living in the future instead of the present moment. You worry that there is not enough time to fulfil all your desires and that others are getting there before you.

In the earth world there are time constraints. But in the spiritual world it is timeless. One of your earth lives is only equal to a few moments in our world. Come, I will take you on a journey."

So saying she holds out here hands and takes you with her into the sky. You travel for a while over the sea before you see in the distance a rugged hill with many people climbing to the peak.

"The people on the lower part of the hill wish they were halfway up the hill and the people half way up the hill wish that they were at the top. Some of those at the top have seen enough and want to be on the bottom again. So you see the human condition is to be rarely satisfied."

This seems to be very true and very amusing to you so you laugh.

"Life is full of choices and if you choose one thing then you have to let the other go. You won't know what the other path might have been but human beings still wonder."

"That's very true." You tell her. "I'll always wonder if my life might have worked out differently. But things move so slowly" You complain.

"The earth plane is a place where you can manifest things." The Angel tells you. "But it takes time so that you can handle the changes. Think of something you want." She advises.

Immediately you think of a bowl of cereal. Suddenly the bowl appears before you suspended in mid air.

"That is amazing!" You tell her.

"It is simple. You wished for the bowl and manifested it. Now imagine something bigger that you want. Say to be the head of a corporation, for instance."

She snaps her fingers and you find yourself in a boardroom. You are the head of the table in a pin stripe suit and dozens of people are asking you questions and to sign documents. The Angel stands behind your chair but they can't see her. You haven't got a clue what they are talking about and you start to panic.

"Take it away! Make them leave!" You beg her.

"Confusing isn't it." She smiles. "You haven't had a chance to prepare. You need what?"

"Time!" You say emphatically.

"Absolutely!" she agrees. "Now say you wanted to meet your perfect partner immediately. Clap your hands."

You clap them and suddenly you are married with three kids. The person sitting in the front room is a stranger to you."

"But I don't know this person!" You complain to the Angel.

To get to know them what do you need?" She asks.

"Time....I need...oh I get it." You answer.

"There you are. There are lots of other things like that. There are also times in our lives when we are learning very important lessons and it feels like nothing is happening. But you are learning something... sometimes on a subconscious level you are being prepared for something in your life. This is a time to be patient with yourself. Lets go somewhere else."

The scene changes and you find yourself suspended in space in a universe with a pink sky behind you. Planets and stars are dotted around the heavens but there is an unreal, ethereal quality to everything. The Angel is suspended in space next to you.

"This is the dimension of Endless Time. This is the place where you visit before you come to the earth place and decide on the course of your life and what you will be learning along with your guides and the creator. It is a place of infinite possibilities."

"With so many possibilities it is so hard to choose." You tell her. "But Angels seem so patient."

"Angels are patient because they understand that everything unfolds in it's own time. It takes trust to have patience. Trust that you have turned your affairs over to a higher guide. With age comes wisdom. Patience often teaches you to learn from the mistakes you made and then you can go out and win. Patience and persistence are not easy

lessons but they both rely on trusting that everything is going to be all right in the end. Just as you are having patience with yourself also have patience with others. Everyone is at a different place on the journey. Some stay in the same habits for years before changing and some refuse to change. Some wait for a crisis to change. Of course we see all of ourselves reflected in others and that can be very annoying. Remember what we see in others are often things we don't like in ourselves. Enjoy the journey. It isn't just arriving. It is also the quality and textures of your life as you go through it. Now it is time to take you back to the Garden of Contemplation." She says and even through you travel slowly you feel refreshed when you arrive there. As you reach the bench she hands you a piece of paper.

You turn to say good-bye but she has already started to fade into the yellow light. But her features are still visible.

"Remember..." She says. "take it slowly." Then she disappears. You read her affirmation.

Affirmation:

I now have infinite patience with everyone and myself in my life.

Beauty
The Angel of Inner Radiance

As you sit in the Garden of Contemplation thinking of your adventures so far in the world of the Angels you realise that although you haven't noticed time passing you see that it is early morning. A gentle light filters through the trees and a warm sun rises above the pond, shining glittering reflections in the water. Birds sing to each other and you listen to one that could rival a soprano. Then you notice a gold hummingbird hovering near some silver lilies.

Further in the forest beyond the garden a deer and fawn leisurely meander through the trees. In the midst of all this wonder you see a rainbow that has formed close to the ground near to where you are sitting. It has stunning colours and you watch in fascination as it changes into a lovely Angel with robes of every colour and iridescent wings.

"Greetings." She tells you and you notice she talks in a soft ethereal whisper. You are amazed but not sure what to make of her. "I am the Angel of Inner Radiance. We have heard that you have sometimes become too stressed to appreciate the beauty of the world around you so I am here to take you on an adventure. We will go to the Temple of Beauty and you will learn about how you relate to your exterior appearance."

"Come," She says, "I will open your eyes to the beauty all around you." Taking your hand she leads you through gardens to the edge of the forest. Here her wings unfold and she pulls you into the sky with her. You fly effortlessly, although this is still new and amazing to you. Beneath you the forest treetops sway in the sunlight. The blue sky is the perfect backdrop for the morning sun, which warms your face and lights the lands beneath you. Suddenly the forest ends and you see the now familiar buildings of the world of the Angels in a rich turquoise sea glowing under a rainbow of colours in a fiery sunrise and you realise that everywhere you are surrounded with beauty. Pinks, pale purples, fiery orange and soft, buttery golden yellow light the sky and spread their beauty over the water.

In the distance lies another temple that shines pale purple and gold in the early light.

"There is the Temple of Beauty." The Angel tells you.

You begin to feel nervous. Is this going to be some strange place where everyone is perfect except for you? You have always had some insecurities about your appearance and, as the temple gets closer, they become magnified. The Angel turns to you and smiles as if she can read your thoughts.

"In the spirit world the beauty of the spirit is what is seen. The goodness and beauty of each soul shines like a beacon and there is no judgement. Beauty can inspire us and take us to higher levels of spirituality. Have you noticed that when you are in love or happy you seem to glow? As you raise your vibration of love and open your heart to more healing then this will send messages to all the cells in your body to wake up and celebrate. You will feel more harmony and happiness".

It sounds too good to be true you think as the land of the Angels is already full of beauty and you wonder what more the Temple of Beauty can give you. But as you travel forward towards the temple you sense that you feel more aware of the beauty that is visible. Looking around at the animals, birds and flowers you perceive an aura of light and colour around everything.

The Angel guides you both to the steps of the temple where graceful columns mark the entrance. Above the columns is an inscription. It says 'The Temple of Beauty'.

As you climb the cool marble steps to the Temple entrance a soft breeze blows your hair and face as if in caress. You feel a stirring of something sweet and long forgotten deep inside you...a yearning a blossoming. Entering the Temple your senses are stirred and almost overwhelmed by the lushness of everything within.

As you enter the palace you notice it is a long hall with marble floors and huge French windows that open onto the surrounding gardens. You see that the ceiling is built out of coloured crystals. Sunlight filters through stained crystal on the ceiling. Everything and everyone here is a feast for the senses. The walls are full of art, rich with vivid hues and evocative scenes. The most incredible music that touches your soul can be heard while nature blooms everywhere...flowers of indescribable beauty and through a doorway a courtyard can be seen with fountains and trees. Everything in this place is full of a beauty that feeds your soul.

Looking around, your heart sinks as you see there are dozens of people here and all of them are looking handsome or pretty. You feel intimidated.

BEAUTY

"What you see is deceiving." The Angel tells you. "This place is a centre of healing for those with problems of low self-esteem because of their appearances. They all come here to look in the magical mirror. Beauty is also how you feel about yourself. In your society you are obsessed with beauty but often in an unhealthy way. There is an obsession with youth and a fear of ageing. Yet each age brings its own gifts if we are open to them. A deep wisdom and tolerance from an older person can be beautiful." She says. "Have you ever known someone who was physically unattractive or ordinary but the love they emanated made their imperfections disappear?

You nod. Then you think of something else. "How do they get here?" You ask her remembering your journey.

"Either at night in their dreams or by astral travelling." The Angel tells you in her soft voice. "Astral travelling means that their awareness can travel to another place or dimension."

You notice the walls are covered in lilac silk and you notice many full length gilt framed mirrors on those walls. She takes you to a huge mirror in an ornate gold frame. You notice that people are lining up to look inside the mirror, gasping in delight and disbelief and then moving on.

"This is a magical mirror." She tells you. "What people see in the mirror is the beauty of their souls".

It all sounds very complicated you decide as you take your place in the queue. But then your own journey to the Land of Angels has been unorthodox. You pass a mirror yourself and glance at it and as the light gently touches your face and as you gaze at your reflection you are amazed at what you see. All of your imperfections have disappeared leaving only the beautiful, loving being that you are. You see yourself as if you have never seen yourself before looking with total love and acceptance. You see your own beauty and all the gifts you bring to your life and all the love you bring to the world. You realise that you feel good about yourself.

"You have become your higher self a pure spirit of light and love. Let the healing take place and know that you will always be aware of this beauty." The Angel tells you.

Now you notice some of the people around you. They are almost transparent. They glow from within. Their inner lights shine so brightly that you can see the beauty of their soul. You realise that you know some of these people. They greet you and you notice a rainbow colour of light streaming from their heart centre.

"it is time to leave, say goodbye to your friends" The Angel says.

Then the Angel takes you by the hand and leads you back over the ocean to a city. As you fly closer you realise it is the city you live in. You fly into the window of your workplace and see the people you work with.

"We can't get anything on the outside we don't have internally first. This becomes more apparent as we become older. Your habits and thoughts become more evident in your body. What you think about perpetually you become - if you worry or sneer constantly as you get older your face will become ingrained by your expressions which come from your thoughts. Looking at older people's faces you can sense what kinds of thoughts they habitually think. Do you want your later years to be a source of worry - a desperate longing for the return of youth - or a maturing...a wisdom welcoming the years as an ageing tree does growing in depth and height and reaching it's branches to embrace the wide world? All of these things are a call for love. We want others to love us - sometimes the love we aren't willing or able to give to ourselves. But others merely mirror our own beliefs about ourselves. If we are relaxed about how we look and focus on that then the outside will reflect that."

As you listen to her you find that you subtly let go of judgements about how people should look. "Many of those people in the palace were one's you judged not beautiful by earth standards but, in the Angel's palace, they are radiant. If you look into anyone's eyes you will see the beauty of their souls." The Angel tells you. "Try it and, using some of your imagination, it works. All are crying out o be accepted and appreciated."

You think of a situation you would have judged before but now you can let go of that conditioning.

She smiles as she reads your thoughts. "Now you know that."

She guides you out of the room and out of the temple.

"Now it is time to return to the garden." She says in her singsong voice.

The Angel takes your hand and suddenly you find yourself drifting through the open window of the Temple and flying...flying over the ocean.

As she takes your hand and you begin to fly you feel an immense joy. Your insecurities about any part of your appearance appear to have gone and all you remember is the beauty of your inner self. As you fly around feeling free and beautiful you can send love to everyone because you feel so good about yourself.

Then you realise that the Angel is speaking to you again. "There are many ways we can connect with beauty. Try to think how you can you create more beauty in the world? As you meditate on this ideas will happen. Have a beauty day. Just one day think beautiful thoughts. Feel beautiful - be somewhere you feel in touch with the beauty of nature - somewhere that feeds your soul. Whatever you focus on grows and as you focus on your own beauty it will grow. As you see the divine part of yourself and you discover your role in the healing of this planet - then your beauty will grow and you won't even notice it."

Soon you alight in the grounds of the palace by the bench.

"Now I must bid you goodbye. Please remember what you have seen. Keep well." The Angel tells you and smiles. As she leaves she hands you a piece of paper with an affirmation:

Affirmation:

Today let me see the beauty in all things including myself.

Her body transforms into a rainbow, which fades leaving a golden glow.

Protection
The Angel of Guardianship

In the Garden on Contemplation time seems suspended and you don't realise that you have been sitting on the bench for a while. You decide to stretch you legs. You get up and walk over the cobbled stones around the fountain. For a while you watch the water cascade into the stone basin.

Suddenly you realise you can hear someone crying. It sounds like a child. Looking at the lawn that leads to the woods you see a small boy of six or seven rubbing his eyes and whimpering. It is a very moving sight. You just start to move towards the child when an Angel with brown curly hair and huge wings swoops down, picks up the boy and flies into the air. As she flies her wings wrap protectively around him. She flies straight upwards towards a beam of light shining on her from the sky. Around the light you can see radiant rainbow colours.

Then she and the boy disappear.

Amazed by the sight you start to return to the bench with your head full of questions. Who was the boy? Why was he crying? Where was the Angel taking him? Just as you reach the bench there is another loud swishing sound and you turn to see the same Angel standing near you. "Sorry about that. The boy was in the wrong place and I had to take him where he belonged." You notice she is talking with a slight New York accent.

"You are from New York?" You ask feeling a bid odd asking this.

"Yeah, I spent a lotta time there. Kinda picked up the accent."

You are longing to ask a question.

"Who was that child?"

"He was the spirit of a boy who just died. When children die they come into the spirit world and they are taken care of by us and other guardians. He was missing his life on earth but now he is with the other children. I'll be visiting him. But at the moment I'm here for you. Hi, I'm the Angel of Protection. I've been hearing about you. You are doing really well! In fact I'm here to give you a lesson in being a guardian Angel!"

As she says this you feel a tickling sensation on your back. It makes you a bit nervous.

"What's going on?"

She giggles. She waves her hands and makes a few signs and you feel small wings on your back.

"They are trainers." She laughs. "Now you can fly by yourself. I'm going to show you what it is like to be a guardian Angel."

This sounds very exciting to you and you can't wait to begin.

"Great." You tell her.

"Hey, lets go." She says. "We're going back to the earth and I want you to be with one person in particular. They won't be able to see you but they will be able to feel your energy."

You fly to the earth, to a crowded city and follow The Angel of Protection to the top floor of a run down apartment building. You fly through an open window. In a threadbare armchair a woman sits crying while a baby sleeps on a sofa.

"This woman is really lonely and sad. She needs help. She has just lost her husband and feels she cannot cope." The Angel informs you. "We are here to give her comfort and strength to go on."

"But she cannot see us." You protest.

"She will feel our energy and one day, when she is open enough, she may see us."

She moves to the woman and embraces her. You go to her and hold the woman's hand. The woman's crying lessens a little and you can feel she is gaining strength.

"Alright now you take over. I'll be back in a few days to see how you are doing." The Angel tells you.

At first you feel panicky when the Angel leaves. But over the next few days you are with the woman day and night. You follow her through the process of trying to find a job to support herself and her baby. You see her struggles, her despair and finally the dawn of new hope. You give her comfort and you sense she feels your energy. You give her healing and send telepathic thoughts of hope and love. You whisper encouragement and suggestions of how to improve her life and she often accepts them as if they were her ideas. The child can see you and waves and gurgles happily at you. Then one night the woman sits up in bed and sees you in her room. She whispers thank you and goes back to sleep contentedly. The next day she wonders if it was a dream. The Angel comes to see you.

"Hey, you've done a great job. Her life is improving now. Thank you. Your work here is done and another will take over. You may go back

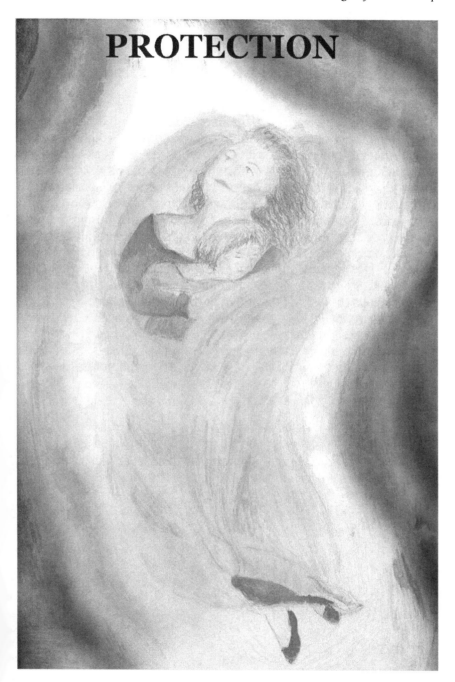

PROTECTION

to the palace. Have you learned a lot?"

You think about it. "Yes," You tell her " I've learned that we all affect each other in many ways even if invisibly. I've learned that when I give love and support I'm not in my ego and thinking about myself, what I want and need."

"All that in a few days! Great!

As she says these words you are back in the palace gardens and you enter the Garden of Contemplation to think about all you have seen.

The Angel is very pleased with you. "When you get back to the earth you can continue." She says. " If you like you could pick someone you know who is in trouble and decide you will be their Guardian Angel. Offer your help and services. Be thoughtful and find ways you can help. Be a good friend and listen to them without judgment. Help them see themselves in a better light and try to lighten whatever they are going through. Pray for them or include them in your meditations. Have a vision of their success and let them know about it and believe in it as well. Your enthusiasm will be infectious. Even if you are not sure how to help above all just accept and love them. That will lead you to the right steps to take to help them. Well you gotta go back now. But it's been great meeting you."

It sounds like a big task and you have a lot to think about as you sit in the garden and wait for the next Angel. Then you notice the slip of paper she left.

Affirmation:

I enfold my Angelic wings of light around those who need it and send them nourishing energy of love so they can feel Spirit's love for them.

Wisdom
The Angel of Deeper Wisdom

You are so deep in contemplation enjoying the sweet smelling roses and the sunlight through the trees and on the water that you are slightly startled when the door to the Angel's Palace is opened and Hera, the Angel in purple robes with stars who met you at the door when you arrived, glides down the marble steps and joins you in the garden. She is wearing robes of deep violet purple and looking down you realize your robes have changed to the same colour.

"Hello again." She smiles.

"Greetings Hera." You find yourself smiling back. She seems mysterious with her purple orb and misty, far away smile.

"My child you are doing so well." She touches your shoulders. " Today I will be taking you to various places to learn about wisdom. The journey begins in the Angel palace. Does that sound good?"

"It sounds very interesting. " You tell her.

"Then follow me."

You follow her up the steps of the Angel's Palace. Her dress of stars is so long that is trailed on the steps after her. You are fascinated, as the stars seem to shine. Then you both go through the ornate wood door. She leads you down a marble floored corridor to oak doors with a sign above them that says: "The Halls of Wisdom"

As she opens the doors you gasp in amazement. Before you is an immense library built in a gothic style that resembles a cathedral. Countless books live in the white wood panelled shelves and light filters through a stained glass window at the far end. Domed Cathedral ceilings give a wonderful feeling of height and you marvel at the rich atmosphere of learning. It is a busy place as well with various people reading at tables.

"These the Halls of Wisdom. All knowledge is contained here. Not only do we have books but if you ask a question in your mind you will telepathically receive the answer." She tells you. "Sort of a psychic internet. Go ahead! Try it! Ask something that you didn't know!"

Thinking hard, you silently ask what is the capital of Peru?

Although you are aware that you don't know the answer it immediately pops into your mind.

"This knowledge is important and valid." She tells you. "But there is another type of wisdom I would like you to aware of. Come, we will be travelling a short distance."

Instead of taking you out of the front door she leads you to a balcony next to the stained glass window. The balcony has a set of French windows that open on to the sea. Leading you through the French windows you see her golden, white and purple wings touched with pink unfold. She takes your hand and flies into the sky taking you with her. As you fly over the treetops you feel the world opening her secrets of wisdom to you. It feels exciting. What mysteries might unfurl before you? You realise that for a long time you have wanted knowledge. Not just book learning but you have wanted to understand why things are the way they are. You have wanted deeper insights into the mysteries of life in the earth plane. Questions such as where do we go when we die? What is the purpose of life? They have bothered you for a long time. Now you feel as if you are on a journey, an invisible journey of learning. Somehow you know that. You sense that this is why you have been chosen by the Angels to come here and to be treated as their special guest and to learn some of their secrets. All that you have done in your life up until this point led you to this place and this place is perfectly right place for you to be. You feel deeply honoured.

The Angel of Wisdom smiles as if she knows what you are experiencing. "Your intuition and third eye are opening." She tells you. "You will be receiving intuitive wisdom about many things. Just accept them even if you don't understand them at once. They may make sense later."

The flying is slowing down and you recognize the Mountains of Wisdom from earlier but you are surprised to see what looks like an ashram at the top of one of the peaks. As you fly closer you can discern the structure and the words 'Psychic School'.

"Here people come to tune out of the noise of the world and get in touch with their intuition and psychic abilities." She tells you. " I will be leaving you here for a while."

In the school you are welcomed. It is a mealtime and you sit at the plain wood benches and tables and enjoy a meal. Then you return to the room to sit in silence. You are asked to try and get in touch with your intuition and inner guidance. What is it telling you?

"You know it is from your higher self if the message is to better yourself or others." The teacher says.

WISDOM

You learn that these teachers are masters who dedicated their lives to spiritual wisdom and progress. One of the teachers takes you aside and explains to you what is going on.

"In Buddhism they talk about thinking correctly saying the right thing and living correctly. Here we meditate to gain wisdom and intuition from the higher part of ourselves. We seek to raise awareness in ourselves so that we understand the true nature of the universe. That is sometimes called enlightenment. Buddha meditated until he gained enlightenment and learned that true wisdom is knowing when to do the right thing for the good of all concerned. It is letting go of the ego. It is striving to make the world a better place than you found it. All the great sages and teachers understood this." He tells you. "Try to discover what is right for you next. Close your eyes. Focus on your breathing and relax."

As you sit in silence with the teacher and, at first, nothing happens. Then you receive a message from your inner guidance. It tells you something important that can help your life.

Afterward you go into the common room and meet other students. They talk about their meditations and various experiences they have. Soon Hera joins you again.

"Getting in touch with your inner guidance is the first step to connecting with psychic abilities. As you develop more then new worlds will open to you." She smiles. "But for now it is time for you to return to the garden."

As she says those words she reaches out her hand. You say your good byes and then take her hand. You both walk to a window where you fly into the sky and back to the Garden of Contemplation. As you arrive back at the bench you feel relaxed and refreshed.

"Sit and think of what you a have learned. " Hera tells you. "I will see you again."

With that she moves towards the steps of the temple. As she leaves you notice a scrap of paper on the bench. You open it up to reveal an affirmation.

Affirmation:

Today I listen to my inner wisdom.

Awakening
The Angel of Remembrance

The Angel of Remembrance appears out of a small pinhole of light that magnifies in front of you to a brilliant white light that is so dazzling you need to almost shield your eyes. Then the light softens and you see a warm, calm face smiling at you.

"I am the Angel of Remembrance. I want to take you with me on my journeys to bring people back into the spirit world. It is time for them to remember the place that they left before their time on earth."

In an instant you are in a cottage near a lake where an old man is lying on a couch obviously breathing his last. He is alone and you feel for him.

"He cannot see me at the moment but soon he will." She tells you. As his body breathes its last his spirit, youthful and fresh, leaves his body and sees the Angel of Remembrance.

"Greetings. Welcome again to the spirit world." She says to him.

He seems joyful and a bit bewildered by your presence. Then you see other spirits have gathered close by to greet him.

"These are his relatives and friends who have passed on before him." She tells you. It is very moving to witness the joy of reunion between everyone.

"Now you can help me with others who are ready to awaken to their new life." She tells you.

Suddenly you are in a family home where a lovely dog, a spaniel, lies unwell. As it closes its eyes and breathes it's last breath, you see the spaniel's spirit leave its body. The spirit is young and vibrant. It looks up at you and wags its tail. It goes around the various family members who are crying but they can't see it.

"Come to the light, Charlie!" The Angel encourages the dog. But the dog doesn't want to leave the family and the love it has known.

"Very often the spirit will stay around the loved ones for a while not wanting to be parted from them. Even when the person or animal goes to what you call heaven then it can return to visit the loved ones any time. There is also communication between the spirit that has gone and the people on the earth plane. You can talk to the departed ones and they can hear you."

"Right away?" You ask.

"No. There is a period of adjustment as their spirit gets used to its new life and remembers life in the spirit world."

You take in her words as you watch the family mourn their beloved pet. You feel sad as you can see the small dog dance around the family who are crying but can't see him. You think of the sombreness of the funeral services when the spirits you have seen are young and happy and the spirit world is so beautiful.

"What about ghosts?" You ask.

"Sometimes spirits get stuck in a place on the earth for various reasons and can't or won't move on. Sometimes they don't realise they have passed on." She tells you. Let's go on."

The noise of a battlefield vibrates in your ears and before you are the horrors or war. You recognise it as the American Civil War. On the television you have seen old photos of the war but now you are in it.

"Look." The Angel says pointing to some of the dead on the battlefield. You see the spirits of the men leaving their body. They are confused. Other spirits are there to help them to the light.

"Each person has learned something from their life...something that was meant for them to learn." The Angel tells you.

"What could anyone possibly learn from being killed in battle?" You ask in horror.

"Many things, depending on the individual." She tells you. They may learn sacrifice for their country or they may learn that violence is not a solution. Every lesson shapes the spirit to wisdom and improvement."

"There seems so much that we don't know and are not allowed to know." You comment.

"Yes that is true. Now it is time for you to return to the Garden and to think about what you have seen." She tells you. With that you are back in the Garden and feel that so much has happened since you were last there although in fact it is only a few hours. On the bench is a scrap of paper.

Affirmation:

I awaken to awareness of the spirit world. Let me be a channel for Divine Light and Love and send it wherever it is needed.

AWAKENING

49

Appreciation
The Angel of Gratitude

From far away you hear the distant sound of sleigh bells. The sky has darkened and through the clouds you can see it has turned midnight blue. Then, although it is hard for you to believe, snow has started to fall in the Garden of Contemplation. It touches your face like frozen kisses. It falls on the ground and you sense Christmas in the air, the season of celebration joy and love. You can hear carollers in the woods and sense their happiness. You feel your own oneness with the earth and with the people around you. Closing your eyes you revel in the heady sensation. You don't feel cold, you feel excited. Then, as the snow begins to fall more heavily, a lovely white sleigh drawn by a single reindeer appears. In the front seat is an Angel with long golden hair crowned by a wreath of holly. She wears vivid, Christmassy colours. She reminds you of winter holidays and the feeling of excitement.

"Get in!" She tells you.

"I'm not sure..." You say looking at the delicate driving seat.

"Come on! Get in! " She urges merrily.

You sit on the red velvet padded seat next to her and the sleigh takes off at an alarming pace. The Angel is obviously enjoying herself. Her long hair is flying out behind her and her blue eyes sparkle happily.

"Er...aren't you an Angel? Don't you fly with wings?" You ask her.

"Oh yes." She waves her hand dismissively. "I just love to travel like this. It makes me feel that it's Christmas: the happiest time on earth!" She laughs and you wonder if she isn't a bit eccentric.

"Let me introduce myself!" She laughs "I'm the Angel of Gratitude and I'm here to talk to you about appreciation. You see I'm the one who travels the world seeing how grateful people are for what they have. Gratitude is a wonderful thing! If you are grateful for small things then you can enjoy life so much more. Many yearn for massive things in their lives and miss the simple blessings that are right under their noses!"

The reindeer moves at an alarming pace over the forests and waterways. Then he takes a sharp turn to the left and you see a planet in the distance.

APPRECIATION

"Where are we going?"

"Back to earth of course!" She smiles "I want to show you some examples of what I'm talking about. First let me take you somewhere where there is no appreciation."

The reindeer picks up speed as you break into the earth's sky and go full speed towards a major city. You wonder if the reindeer has got it's driving license as the journey is rather bumpy but the Angel doesn't seem to notice. Waking from your reverie you find yourself on the roof of a massive mansion in a fashionable part of town.

"Alas the reindeer can't help us now...I need to use magic. Hang on." She says and then you are in the living room with a man talking rapidly on his phone. He seems angry.

"This man has everything but appreciates nothing. He feels he has bought his wife and does need to give her affection. He has sent his kids to boarding school so they won't be noisy in the house and anyone that works for him he despises because he can manipulate them. His only redeeming feature is that he loves his cat."

You laugh as a large ginger cat jumps on his lap as he studies his figures on his computer.

"Life is about to send him a lesson. Over the next few years he will lose everything."

You fast forward to a few years later and he has lost everything in a stock market crash and bad investment deals. His wife has left with another man who appreciates her and has taken the kids with her. His house has been repossessed as he had to re-mortgage it for a deal and the cars have been sold to pay for debts.

"I suppose he didn't appreciate what he had." You question her. So are you saying money is evil?"

"Not at all." She says. "Look at this." She takes you to a charity benefit where a wealthy woman has raised a lot for charity.

"That woman works tirelessly to help other and feels glad that her money is doing good. Money itself isn't bed or good. It is how people view it and what they do with it. The lady next door is equally wealthy but spends a lot of her time and money helping others.

"Sadly greed has a hold on the world. Humility and gratitude are very spiritually linked and are the opposite of greed. For the greedy person there is never enough no matter what they have. Yet there is no judgement. Only lessons that they will understand one day."

"Now I will take you to someone who is appreciative. " She tells you. You travel over the rooftops of a city in winter. The rooftops are covered with snow and you do feel like Father Christmas and wish you had a few presents to pop down the chimneys.

The Angel jingles the reins slightly, the sleigh bells sing a pretty sound and the reindeer weaves its way through the houses until it stops outside the window of a run down house in a poor district.

"Look inside." The Angel tells you.

Inside the window a young woman rearranges her belongings. Obviously underfed she nevertheless exhibits a cheerful countenance as she sings merrily to herself while decorating her room with a few sprigs of holly and tinsel.

"This woman can barely pay the rent with her job as a waitress. She is alone in the world yet her gratitude and selflessness have won her many friends. Tomorrow is Christmas and she is going with a group who are feeding the homeless. She does this every year and by the end of the day she will feel richer than the millionaire has ever felt. Riches are not in the bank but in the heart." The Angel tells you.

"She has a beautiful voice!" You exclaim. She could be a professional singer with such a voice!"

The Angel nods. "Because of all her hard work she will be heard by a theatre owner who can offer her work as a singer. She will rise though the ranks and be successful. But success will not change her kind nature."

"Now lets get to your life." She says.

"Let's not." You tell her.

In an instant you find yourself in your home. The Angel of Appreciation shows you different areas of your life and how lucky you are.

"Whatever you focus on, your energy grows.. Look at this!" She says and you see a diagram of the energy of gratitude going from someone's heart and out into the universe and drawing even more good things towards the person.

"Focus on the positive! When was the last time you looked around your life and really gave thanks for all the blessings you already posses? We don't have to wait for things to be 'perfect' before we start being happy and grateful for what we do have.

Think about the best thing in your life right now - something that you are always grateful for: a child, a spouse, your health, friends, talents abilities everyone has at least one. Give silent thanks.

Now think of five things in the past that you feel you have been blessed by - a wonderful love, a loving family, a moment of success in schoolwork or sports. Say a silent thank you.

Now take a piece of paper and write down all your favourite things - everything from toffee fudge ice cream to your favourite music to Marx Brothers to the colour of the clouds today to the rain to all your friends and loved ones. In short to everything you can think of. Life can be pretty great." She laughs merrily.

"Sadly it is time to return to the garden of Contemplation where you can think about what you have seen."

You are returned to the garden where it is still night time. It has stopped snowing and the white layers are soft on the ground. To you the holiday feeling is still in the air. She deposits you on the steps of the Angel Temple.

"Go inside where it is warm." She tells you.

Then, with a whoosh of snow and the sound of bells the Angel guides the sleigh into the night. "Good bye" She calls as she waves over her shoulder. You wave back to her until she disappears. Then a scrap of paper falls at your feet.

Affirmation:

My heart is overflowing with gratitude as I become aware of all the wonderful gifts in my life.

As you open and read it then it turns into a snowflake which falls and melts on the ground.

Healing
The Angels of Healing

In the Garden the sun is setting once again shooting brilliant rays of colour across the pale peach sky. Deep magenta, cerise pink, orange and lilac spill across the sky like an artist's palette. You still can't get used to how quickly the days and the nights pass here or the intense beauty of the land. A supper has appeared magically on a table near the bench and for some reason you were not surprised to find your favourite dish there.

So lost in a daydream are you that the appearance of two female Angels startles you. They are dressed in pinks and light reds with gold and red wings which seem to match the warmth of their personalities. One is a shorter and a bit rounder and the other tall and slim one.

"Greeting." Says one.

"Greetings." Says the other.

"We are two of the healing Angels." They tell you.

"There are more?" You ask.

"Many more!" One of them laughs. "In fact every Angel has healing abilities just as all humans have healing as well as psychic abilities. They are in different strengths according to how developed they are."

"What are your names?" You ask.

"Oh unpronounceable!" One tells you.

"Totally!" The other says. "But you can call us Martha and Gertie."

"Yes, that will do nicely. I'm Gertie." Says the shorter and slightly rounder of the two.

"Come, we want you to help us with someone who needs healing."

"Me?" You say, surprised. "I can't do anything!"

The Angels laugh. "You don't have to. Just learn to let the healing energies of the universe flow through you. Come."

Evening has fallen. The sky has become a canopy of stars with a brilliant crescent moon shining over the land. The tall Angel takes your hand gently. You feel safe and warm as they lead you to a brick wall covered with ivy. Pulling the ivy aside they reveal a special side door that you haven't noticed before. The two Angels chatter happily to each other as Martha opens the door with a golden key. Down some stone steps you find a small boat in the shape of a swan, standing by the waters edge. The Angels step into the boat and you follow them. As they do their wings move and the boat sails out onto the water.

"But in learning to become a healer the first step is always to balance ourselves. We can't offer wholeness if we do not know on some level how to create it. I think of healing as three areas: Physical, Emotional, Mental and Spiritual. They all affect each other. You can start work on any of them and will also be affecting the others."Gertie tells you.

"They all use the magical ingredient of love." Martha adds "Physical balance means first of all loving and accepting your body as it is. We all have things we don't like about our bodies and it is good to change what you can. Try to make an agreement with yourself that you will treat your body in the most loving way - feeding it with only the purist and healthiest ingredients. "

There are many animals in the sea. You see whales, flying fish and dolphins. They are all friendly and stop to talk to each other and you. You find you understand their language.

"These are healing waters." Martha explains as the boat stops. "Look over the side of the boat."

As you do as she asks you notice the water has become as still as a mirror. By the starlight which has become very bright and the lantern in the boat you can see yourself very clearly. But there is something odd about your appearance. An odd mist of coloured light or energy is around your body and moves as you do. Then in this energy are circles of light at different points over your body. They seem to spin. You notice one above your head, one on your forehead and a blue one at your throat.

"What's wrong with me?" You ask them.

"Nothing." The tall slender one says.

"No, nothing, dear." The other chimes in.

"What you are seeing is your aura. It is the energy field that surrounds your body. The whirls of light are called charkas. The one on your forehead is called your third eye."

You have heard of the third eye and didn't believe it existed.

"Now look at your heart charka, dear. It is above your heart." Gertie says.

It seems to you that you see your reflection - healthier and more radiantly glowing than ever before. Yet around your heart you see some clouds.

HEALING

"This is residue sadness and hurt from past experiences," she explains. "This is lessening the flow of love from your heart to you. This means the flow is lessened to everyone else. It needs healing and balancing I would say."

"Yes, I would, Gertie, indeed I would. Look again in the water, dear. The dolphins will help you." Martha tells you.

"Dear me yes, Martha they are so very wise." Gertie adds.

Again you look over the side of the boat and don't feel surprised to see a dolphin rise from beneath the waves with a golden chalice full of water. Thanking him you reach down and take the cup. The dolphin wishes you luck and healing. Then he dives beneath the waves.

Somehow you know what to do - dipping your fingers in the water you then place your hand over your heart and let the healing take place.

Gently, you feel some old barriers and old pain melting under the magical healing waters. You let it go. Emotion swells up and crashes down like wave on the shore. Sadness...fear...anger...whatever it was it is leaving. A soft pink light begins to glow around your heart area as you feel a gentle love warm you. This light spreads all around you, filling your aura with pink and soft aqua on the edges. You see an image of yourself at your daily business and now you are able to feel more compassion towards yourself. You feel free and wish that everyone you know could experience this magic.

"Now give the chalice back to the dolphin." Gertie tells you.

You hold the chalice above the water and the dolphin reappears takes the chalice, bows to you and disappears again.

"That's good dear." Gertie says. "Now we can go back to the healing centre."

"Yes, dear. Now you've seen your aura and had some healing we can teach you to send healing energy to others."

"But I thought that you said these are the healing waters." You say to them.

"Dear me. Healing can come in many forms." The tall one tells you. "Music, for instance has many healing qualities as does laughter!"

"Ah, yes many are discovering that singing certain notes into the chakras can balance then." Gertie tells you as the boat moves back towards the Angel's Palace. "Then there are other things such as a touch, a smile, a concerned talk and a hug to a healing session from a member of the healing arts. On a subtle level it is said that others receive every thought we think about them on some level. Our energies are either hurting or healing - so it all begins with thinking the most loving thought about yourself and the other person that you are trying to help. Sometimes all people need is to be heard. Being an open listener can be an art where you simply allow people to talk and be there for them with suggestions and positive encouragement. They may have lost their way to loving themselves and are full of self blame or hurt. If you remind them how wonderful they are and keep on until they agree with you then it changes the energy and dynamic of the situation and they start to feel better. Movement again is very beneficial to the emotions. Yoga is wonderful for calming the emotions and relieving stress. Meditation, especially the Tibetan Buddhist form or Zen is very relaxing and contemplative. This is where you sit it in silence observing your breathing. There are many other healing influences: Colours that we wear and that we see affect our moods, our energy and health. Different colours have different energies and it is good to attune ourselves to the right colours for us."

"Oh you do go on so, dear!" Martha says.

"What sort of healing do you both do?" You ask.

"We work with the light." Gertie tells you.

"White light, dear. Very powerful." Martha answers you. "There are healing energies of light that come through the vibration of love. Everyone has access to these energies as everyone has the ability to love and become a channel for healing."

"Just as everyone has psychic abilities but in some it is more developed." Gertie adds. "Anyway it all comes from the same source....you know what we mean dear. Ah here we are."

The boat docks again at the steps and this time as you alight they lead you to another door in the wall. A small stone path bordered by flowers leads to a modest wood door in the Angel's Palace. There is a sign over the door that says: 'Healing Centre'.

Inside you find a high-ceilinged room decorated in muted pastels. Gentle music is playing and the room is lit by torches in the wall that cast soft shadows. There are many people lying on the tables and Angels, sometimes several are around each table are sending healing light to each person.. You are moved by the lovely energy in the room. Everywhere you look people are giving and receiving and the energy is calm and loving in the room.

Martha and Gertie lead you to one of the tables or beds where a young girl is lying asleep.

"Before she slept she asked to be taken to the Halls of Healing." One of the Angels tells you. Anyone can ask. Then, when they sleep they will be brought here and we will give them healing energy. "

"Will she be cured?" You ask.

"That is not up to us. We are merely channels to give love and positive healing energy and that energy will go to where it is needed whether it is mind body or spirit. It will benefit the person but how we cannot say."

"Now place your hands over her. Close your eyes and think loving thoughts. Allow that love to come through you from the Universal healing energies to the person who needs it. Your hands may become warm."

You join them, tuning in to the vibration of healing and love and allow the universal love to go through you and touch the patients.

After the girl there are others to give healing energy to. The Angels then all form a circle and meditate. They hug each other. You feel light with a heady sense of happiness and a deep peace which surprises you.

When it is over, the Angels guide you out of the palace through the entrance of the healing centre. They take you back to the garden. When you return to the Garden it is morning. Despite being up all night you feel refreshed.

"Thank you for your help." Says Gertie, the chubby one.

"Yes, you did well."Martha admits.

"No, you exclaim. Thank you! What a wonderful experience!"

"Well rest now." Martha tells you.

"Yes, replenish yourself. We will be near. "Gertie tells you. "When you return to the earth you might like to learn spiritual healing or Reiki healing to continue what you have learned here."

"Yes, both are good dear." Martha adds.

"Good bye." Gertie says.

"Good bye, dear." Martha waves.

"Good bye. Thank you." You wave to them as they return to the Palace through the side door.

On the table near the bench is a light snack and something to drink. You decide to lie down and take a nap. As you fall asleep you see the scrap of paper on the table. Opening up it reveals an affirmation the healing Angels left for you.

Affirmation:

I allow healing into every area of my life.

Vision
The Angel of Inspiration

It is sunset in the Garden of Contemplation and the sun gently sets in a golden sky casting out crimson and purple hues over the pond and through the trees as it makes way for the night. You feel a slightly nervous at the thought of being in the garden alone but strangely you are not scared. You know that no harm can come to you in this land and that you are a spirit here light and ephemeral.

Suddenly you feel a soft touch on your arm and turn to see a tall, powerful and beautiful male Angel wearing robes of gold and green. His face is old and wise and yet there is a youthfulness about him.

"Good evening. I am the Angel of Inspiration." He says. "Tonight I will take you on a journey to explore the world of visions and inspiration. It is the time for you to get in touch with that unlimited part of yourself. Come, let us explore your visions and dust off your dreams."

Taking you by the hand he leads you through the grounds and over the trees to a small building surrounded by Roman pillars. You enter and find yourself in a room made of crystals. As you enter it the rich colours emanating from the light reflecting through the coloured crystals makes you feel warm and full of possibilities.

"This is the Temple of Inspiration and this is the Room of Dreams and Visions." He tells you and as he speaks you notice one wall is covered with strong, moving rainbow colours and it begins to show giant images like that of a huge video screen. The rainbow colours form into a picture and you see yourself on the screen and you are doing some of the things you love to do.

"These are your hopes and dreams." He says and you realise you are watching the fulfilment of some of your cherished dreams. Have you ever had a glimpse of a lovely place or time drifting past your minds eye? " He asks you. "This is the eternal world of spirit. Have you ever felt the whispers of knowing deep in your heart? This is your guidance gently urging you to open to more light and love or guiding you onwards to the next step of your path. Honour that voice - it could be your Angel visiting." He says. "Angels have a higher vision for you because they can see past a limited earth existence and can see the soul part of you - the higher, beautiful unlimited part that all striving to express."

"What are visions?" You ask him.

"Visions are glimpses of paradise. Visions can be glimpses of the future or another world. They could be a possible or a certain destiny in your path. Of course it could just be your imagination. Visions are seeing with your heart and your imagination. Look"

His words ignite your imagination. You look into the colours and you can see yourself being happy. You can see bright colours of the rainbow around the scene. It is glowing.

"To follow a dream - to act on a vision is very magical and powerful." The Angel tells you. "It has energy because your heart is in it. Too many people give up on their dream. Believe in your dream. It might be your life's purpose and a gift to the world and the limiting part of you does not believe it can manifest it. Take small steps towards it. Don't judge it by time. Give it all the time it needs to manifest. Don't worry about what others think. Following your dream can be scary but it can also be exciting. Outside opinions might tell you that you are too old, too poor, in the wrong place etc. to achieve your dreams. But listen to your inner voice and trust your vision."

The Angel of Vision smiles at you kindly. "Let us now reach your divine spirit of unlimited potential. As you stand there, think of a quality you would like more of in your life or a particular dream. As he waves his wand you see your dream in front of you. "What is blocking you?" He asks "It it a belief? Is it fear? Is it a self consciousness that others might think a certain thing about you? Don't judge yourself - just observe with gentle compassion."

The Angel of Vision touches your heart and you release your doubts and fears. He waves his hand again and a circle of white light appears out of the darkness just above your head. This light has intelligence and feeling. "Ask the light to aid you in letting go of your limitations." He suggests.

You relax as the white light descends around you, surrounding you, bathing you in it's gentle glow. You feel safe and protected and free. This light dissolves any restrictions. You are one with the cosmic energy of love and healing. You can do anything you want. There is an area in your heart and your life you want to heal so you invite this light in - like a treasured friend - and you ask it to do it's magic. And it does. You feel transformed. You walk forward into what it is you want and silently thank the light for being there for you. As you do this the

radiance brightens, splits into rainbow colours and illuminates the room dancing round in celebration. Through the window a golden rain of light falls from the stars and fireworks appear in the sky.

"To be reinspired let go of the negative past. You need to give yourself fresh hope. See it all as part of the past. Part of a perfect learning process you went through. Look towards the future with new vision and trust. Belief is the key to inspiration. We are the creators of our reality and if we hold a vision for what we want and hold that vision through any adversity in our lives then, if it is also for our highest learning and good, we will receive it. It is also important for us to believe we deserve the best - the highest our vision reveals. That is the lesson of self love and worth in our vision. To believe in what has not yet materialized. There is a lot to be said for responsibility but there is always a way, however small to follow your vision and create your dream. Visions can also be a psychic telephone - telling us when someone is in trouble or just needs a call from us. That's when your visions of other people can affect their future.

"Come, "He tells you. "I will show you The Visionary."

Then the Angel of Vision takes your hand and you both fly out through one of the windows and into the night sky. The night sky is heavy with stars and a comet passes overhead You fly over the forests you land in a clearing near a forest of trees. You sense the woodland creatures around you, friendly and curious. Fireflies play amongst the trees as well as the lights of fairies and nature spirits. Then the forest gives way to sand dunes stretching for miles into the sun setting over a shining sea. As you reach the shore the colours of the robes of the Angel of Inspiration's change to a pink. On the dunes you see a tall man with blonde hair standing alone facing the sea. He seems to be watching the sky above the ocean where strange lights are shining and a heart that is formed by the pink clouds.

"This is the Visionary. He lives in solitude here by the beach watching for visions and inspiration from the Angels and guides" The Angel tells you. "He explores the world of spirit and then weaves his creativity with these visions raising his music and art to a higher vibration."

You watch for a while until fireworks explode in wondrous beauty in the sky. As the fireworks end you see a vision in the sky. This is your own private vision. The Angel tells you: "Cherish you vision, nurture is with love and it will grow."

"Come, it is time to return to the garden." The Angel tells you.

As you are flying back he turns to you.

"If you don't have a vision - then look into your heart and see what you love and let your imagination go to the very best outcome. Each step on your journey can be a celebration of opening more to the goodness of the universe." The Angel tells you. "Have a Magic Vision Book. In this you write down every dream, hope, and vision that occurs to you. Write down creative ideas, stories, poems, drawings. Your guides and Angels will help you."

As he returns you to the garden he hands you a slip of paper, then waves goodbye. You read what is on the paper.

Affirmation:

I cherish a positive vision of the future.

Trust
The Angel of Innocence

At first you think it is a beam of sunlight catching your eyes and playing tricks on you. You can see a shaft of golden light as you sit in the Garden of Contemplation listening to the fountains and watching the flowers and trees. Then you see the gold has become two golden wings and an Angel is before you.

"Good morning." She says. "I am the Angel of Innocence. In the spirit world we have heard that you are insecure and that can make you cynical. It also means you sometimes lose your faith. I am here to help you see things differently."

The first thing you notice about the Angel of Innocence is that she is carrying a baby. But this baby also has wings. You realise it must be a baby angel.

"Children have a perfect innocence and trust in the world with a sense of adventure. As you grow you can lose that but if you are in touch with the spirit world then you realise the magic you dreamed about as a child does exist and never leaves you. It is only the body that ages."

Thinking for a moment, you realise that since you have been in the world of the Angels and going on various adventures you have felt excited again and amazed by the magical world you could never have dreamed existed.

"First I want to take you to the eternal universe." She says and a breeze blows your hair as you are lifted up into the air and you find yourself flying alongside her. You realise she hasn't even touched you! You decide she must be a pretty powerful Angel. Looking into her arms you see the baby has fallen asleep from the rocking motion of the flying.

Soon you are out in the cosmic universe and you think it looks familiar and you have visited here before with other Angels.

"This is where creation begins." The Angel explains. "This is where you stood before you went to the earth plane."

Stood, you feel is the wrong choice of phrase as all you are standing on is air and suspended in mid air in the pink night sky. The baby has woken up and it is gurgling and fluttering its small gold wings.

INNOCENCE

"Now!" says the Angel seriously but kindly "Do you remember?"

"Remember what?" You ask but suddenly memories come back to you. Memories of plans made on this very spot. You had planned some events in your life as well as some things you would learn.

Then you realise you and the Angel of innocence are not alone. There are two others here.

"These are your spirit guides." The Angel tells you. Looking at them you feel as if you recognise them from somewhere.

"What is a spirit guide?" You ask.

"They agreed to help you and protect you while you were on the earth plane. Know that you are never alone and there are people who care for you and are watching over you.

You embrace and then they disappear. You feel a great gratitude to them and an amazement that though invisible they will be watching over you.

"Now I want to take you to a time in your earth life that has not happened yet."

The Angel of Innocence tells you. You are going to become yourself in your old age." She snaps her fingers.

Almost instantly you find yourself on a porch in a cosy house in the country. Looking down at your body you see that you are older and sense that you have not a lot of time left on the earth plane.

You sit in your chair on the porch and think of your life. You see the events and remember the emotional journeys of every decade and see the learning and growth you experienced. You see yourself with all your hopes and fears at the age you are now. Knowing, as you do, the future you decide to enjoy your life a little more and know that everything will guide you to learn and experience what you need to. Even the negative, painful events seem part of your life plan.

You then find yourself back in your present body.

"Now it is time for you to return to the Garden of Contemplation." The Angel tells you. The baby has fallen asleep again in her arms as you alight in the garden. There is much to think about as you sit upon the bench.

"Goodbye and I hope this has helped." The Angel says.

"Very much so. Thank you." You tell her.

"Till the next time then." She smiles and starts to turn into the shaft of gold light.

The baby Angel wakes, coos and flutters its wings at you.

"Bye bye..." it says and then they disappear.

Before she leaves she hands you a scrap of parchment with an affirmation on it. You read it slowly.

Affirmation:

I allow the possibility of miracles in my life.

Happiness
The Angel of Joy

You are sitting admiring the beauty of the Garden of Contemplation waiting for another Angel to visit you when a small golden haired child runs past your bench, giggling. You can't tell if it is a boy or a girl as it wears a white shift and gold sandals but the laugh of the golden haired child and the mischievous twinkle in its eye is infectious. You find yourself smiling. It obviously wants a game of chase as it runs around the bench and then stops and looks at you in challenge. Laughing, you stand up and chase after the child at which point it squeels even louder and runs away remarkably quickly for its stubby little legs. It heads into the forest and you, feeling lighter and happier than you have done for a while, give chase, laughing all the while. The trees form a canopy of leaves over your head where the sunlight filters onto the path and the child in front of you twists and turns out of sight so that you can barely see it. Somewhere along the path you realise that you also have become small. Suddenly you stop in front of a mirror that appears seemingly from nowhere and you see yourself and notice that you have become a child as well. You see you are also for a moment semi-transparent. You see joy, like spring of golden energy bubbling up inside you. You are glowing. You look radiant and happy.

Your legs are stubby and your hands tiny. You feel confused but unconcerned as you are still laughing. Not only have you physically become a child but you see that the world looks different to you. All your worldly adult cares and worries have been lifted from you. You feel light and joyful. Life again seems a wonderful adventure and whatever your earthly childhood was like this is a magical childhood in the world of the Angels and you know you are safe to play and explore this kingdom.

Just as you think these thought the path breaks through the trees and you find yourself in a clearing. The small golden cherub is standing by a white horse. Then you realise this is no ordinary horse. It is a unicorn. The child is stroking its mane and talking softly to the beast who seems, amazingly to you, to be talking back.

JOY

"He says he will take us for a ride to wherever we want to go." The child tells you.

Before you have a chance to wonder why the child can speak in such a grown up fashion it talks again.

"Climb on!" It says.

Looking dubiously at the back of the unicorn which has no saddle and towers above you at your present height you wonder how that is possible. But magically a small set of wooden steps appears in front of you and you climb them and gingerly get on its back. Amazingly it feels comfortable!

"Hold onto it's mane! We 're leaving now!" The child says to you.

Before you can ask any more questions two huge wings expand from the side of the horse and it rises into the air taking both of you with on a breathless journey. Although the transition is fairly smooth you feel scared and amazed at the strength of the muscles of the unicorn as they move beneath you, his wings flapping against the air.

Below you is the clearing in the forest that you just left, then in the distance you can see the Garden of Contemplation and the Angel's Palace. The unicorn takes you in a different direction. You travel over the sea. You feel a glory at the sun on your skin and the wind in your face and hair. You feel the thrill of adventure and freedom.

"That is where we are going!" The child points to an island in the ocean.

In a few moments the unicorn lands on the edge of the island as the sun shines over the trees and balmy breezes blow. White sands line the shores and lovely palm trees sway in the wind. It seems like paradise.

You turn to the child to say something and are stunned to see she has become a fully grown Angel with golden hair and blue and lilac robes. Her wings are blue and a ray of white light circles her wherever she goes.

"I am the Angel of Joy."

In her hand is a glowing sphere of white light with a pink heart in it.

"Where are we?" You ask

"This is the island of broken dreams. As a child you believed in the world with the innocence of all children fresh from the world of spirit. You saw the magic and possibilities in the world. Some of that belief is still in you." She says. "These people have had so many bad experiences in life that they are afraid to be happy as it may not last or bring more pain. They are afraid to hope and live in self righteous negativity feeling that if they are negative then they won't be surprised when bad things happen.

"But it is lovely here!" You say.

The Angel shakes her head.

"They refuse to see it and only complain constantly."

"What are we doing here?" You ask.

"Do you see this sphere?" the Angel asks. "When you pass this over their heart then it lifts their worries and they return to the joy and innocence of a child."

The Angel leads you away from the sea, down a path that takes you into a village full of people. As you get closer to the village you can see them in the market place and hear the discordant sounds of their complaining.

You realise that you can hear their thoughts. "They are very negative." You say to the Angel.

"They are very unhappy." The Angel tells you. "Now they won't be able to see us but they should feel the presence of the sphere. Here..."

She hands you the sphere that she is holding. The light momentarily surprises you. It feels warm in your hands and you have a wave of happiness and love wash over you.

"What do I do?" You ask her.

"Hold the light as close to their hearts as you can. It will heal their hurts and remind them of love and joy and that they are safe".

It sounds a tall order as many seem to enjoy exclaiming how terrible everything in life is. Others stand on the outskirts of the group just staring into space despondently.

"Try it on her." The Angel encourages you. You look at where she is pointing and see an older woman in her sixties looking enviously at youngsters playing in the square. You listen to her thoughts.

"I could have been someone important in my life. I never had the opportunity." The woman thinks bitterly.

"Move the light close to her heart." The Angel encourages. "She is a grandmother with a big family that love her but she can't feel lucky."

You move closer to the woman and bring the sphere of light with the heart light in it close to her own heart.

Amazingly the light from the sphere extends out to her heart and somehow the strained muscles of her face relax and she has a faint smile. You can see her whole being change. Her thoughts change.

"I feel content with my life. Life is good and I've been lucky to have so much love." The old woman thinks.

"Well done!" Says the Angel. "Now try that man over there! His wife left him and took the children."

You see a young man of about thirty leaning against a wall. He looks sad. You listen to his thoughts.

"I was in love...but they left me. I'll probably never find love again. Maybe there is something wrong with me."

Gently you bring the sphere of light closer to him and near to his heart. He shudders as the energy hits his heart and looks around for an explanation. Then he smiles and relaxes. A young woman walks past him and smiles. He smiles back. You grin at this promising exchange. You turn to look happily at the Angel. "It's working! Whose next?"

"That woman there. She has just miscarried and feels she will never have children."

Again you move close to the woman and listen to her thoughts.

"All I ever wanted was a family of my own." Her thoughts are. As you get close to her the sphere does its work and she relaxes.

"What am I thinking! There is still time for me!" The young woman thinks.

Over the next few hours you and the Angel work your way around the village. By the time you leave people are happy and talking about an impromptu street party. Their eyes are open to the beauty around them. "Well that was a job well done!" The Angel of Joy tells you as you both travel back to where the unicorn waits. On the beach below the young man is walking with the girl.

"Don't worry. They can't see the unicorn either." The Angel tells you. "Now hop on!"

After patting the soft white nose of the unicorn, who seems to have been content to wait for you for hours, you get on his back and are soon joined by the Angel. The unicorn rises into the air and as you travel over the sea the sun sets and streaks radiant colours over the island.

"Have you learned anything about happiness?" The Angel asks you although her voice sounds younger.

"Yes. It seems that hope is the key to happiness. Those who had lost hope or lived in fear of nothing improving seemed to be in a very negative spiral that took them to where happiness wasn't possible. Life seemed grey and grim."

"Very true."

"It seems to start with being grateful for yourself and who you are and what you have and really just being alive."

"You don't need a reason to be happy. It can just be a choice." The Angel agreed. "Ah. Here we are."

The unicorn alighted on the lawn in the Garden of Contemplation and you alight by the bench where you like to sit. In the Garden it is early morning.

As you turn to thank the Angel you see she has turned back into a laughing child that waves to you as the unicorn lifts into the sky. A scrap of paper falls at your feet.

"Farewell. We can live joyfully whenever we focus on it, decide upon it, and take the steps to bring it into out lives. Remember to be happy."

Affirmation:

I now choose to create more joy in every area of my life.

Compassion
The Angel of Compassion

You wake from a sleep in the Garden of Contemplation to hear someone calling your name. A voice leads you to a secret path in the garden. At the end of the long path you have never visited before you discover a small, domed temple like structure supported by classic columns. A stone bench by one of the columns has a soft cushion on it. You decide to sit for a while. You are enjoying the peace and harmony there and the sweet smelling roses when a gentle murmur of music and soft but startling wind moves past you. As you turn you see another Angel had joined you. This one's yet different again from all the rest and you are awed and stand in wonder at her appearance.

Dressed simply, wearing a crown of golden stars this Angel has huge golden wings that are nearly as tall as she is. White and blue beams radiate from her and she stands with her hands in prayer.
You feel a wave of peace and love in her presence.

She bows to you with her hands still in prayer and you do the same. Then she talks to you. But you realise she is talking telepathically.

"I am the Angel of Compassion and I am here to take you back to the earth to experience with more understanding and compassion with your fellow man."

What is compassion? You ask her.

"Compassion could be said to be seeing the suffering of another and feeling empathy. " She tells you. "It may be their situation or within themselves, even if the suffering is self-inflicted, compassion is recognising the struggles we all face, the shortcomings that create our humanity, and not blaming but understanding and also realising that "there but for the grace of God" could have been you. Compassion is seeing the basic humanness in another person. It is seeing that they are doing the very best they can, even if their actions are hurting others." She tells you.

"Getting in touch with our own compassion for another often begins with learning to be compassionate within ourselves. How can we extend to another what we are unable to muster within ourselves?

COMPASSION

"Learning to be compassionate with yourself means first of all understanding in what areas you are critical or angry with yourself. Did you have a critical parent? A critical teacher? Try and find out whose voice it is who is less that compassionate to you: Only through giving love and compassion, those very qualities, to ourselves first of all. If we are needy, in pain, or feeling isolated and unworthy how can we feel connected to anything else?"

You feel this is going to be an unusual experience so you nod and send your thoughts back to her.

"Thank you."

"Let us begin." The Angel says telepathically, and before you can wonder how you will both reach the earth, you find yourself transported to the inside of a bank. It is a busy day and the office personnel are running around or working hard on the computer and the teller windows. One man, obviously the manager, is barking orders and rushing around in a sweat. He seems a surly, middle aged person in a dark suite with a permanent scowl.

You have nearly forgotten the Angel next to you when her light, telepathic thoughts interrupt you.

"This is the man you will become for a brief time" She tells you." Come."

You both follow the man who returns to his office and is staring at some printed paper on his desk. You are wondering what she means that you will become him when you feel a push, like hands on your back as you leap into the man's body. Your first thought is that it is not pleasant. His ideas and emotions are churning with rage and pain like a washing machine on full cycle. You wonder at the source of his torment. On his desk are a few photos in a frame. A woman smiles at the camera with her arms around two young boys of about ten. As you experience the bank managers thoughts he remembers the long protracted illness of his wife and his grief that alienated his sons. He has not been able to resolve the grief or heal the rift with his boys who are now fully grown. Immediately you feel sad for his suffering and wonder what can be done to help him. The Angels voice breaks into your thoughts.

"Call this number." You see a telephone number appear on a pad in front of you. You use the telephone and did not sure what you will find.

"Hello?" You ask.

"Dad?" A very surprised voice answers.

"Son." You wonder what you can say. "Listen I've called to...

Again the Angel interrupts.

"Say that you are miss him and invite him and his brother to dine with you on Sunday."

You do so.

"Eh, yes. That would be great. I'll tell Tom."

As you replace the receiver you find yourself out of his body and back in your own.

"Isn't that interfering?" You silently ask the Angel as you both watch the man.

"He wanted to make the call." The Angel tells you. "He just lacked the strength. Look, he's glad he called now and believes that he did it."

The man is indeed smiling.

The scene disappears. You find yourself in a parked caravan in a residential area. Opposite you is a girl at a table eating a box of chocolates and reading a romance novel. Very quickly you find yourself in the girl's body. You experience her thoughts and feelings.

"This girl has not been out much during the last 10 years." The Angel tells you.

You become aware of the girls memories and an overwhelming fear and paranoia. She is someone you might have judged before but experiencing her fear of the outside world you have compassion for her.

"Why is she so fearful?" You ask the Angel.

"Her mother was full of many fears taking the girl out of school and keeping her at home. Slowly she picked up her mother's fears." The Angel pauses. "She also experienced a certain amount of abuse when she was young and that has also made her fearful of the world. Why don't you try stepping outside the caravan?"

Opening the caravan door you become aware of the thoughts of self-hatred the girl has for herself because of her weight. It seems sad to you that people constantly seem to torture themselves mentally.

"The secret to keeping our heart open is through loving and nurturing ourselves. Having compassion for our own weaknesses leads us to acceptance. Then other people's struggles are a mirror of our own."

You take a few steps outside of the caravan and try to send the girl thoughts of safety and security. You try to focus on the beauty of the day. You feel the girl relax. You hope that you have planted some positive thoughts in her mind.

Then you are out of her body.

"Now you think of one person in your own life...someone you have not understood before or empathised with. For a moment you can become them. Just feel what it is like. Just imagine the hopes and pressures that they face." The Angel says to you. "Can you let your heart open a little more for them? Is there anything you can do to help lighten their load? Make a call...send a note...let them know that you care. The more you give to others the more returns to you and the more love you find you have to give. "

The scene changes. Now you find yourself watching someone you know. It is someone you have judged before. Then, for a few moments, you step into their life. You experience what it is like to be them and to have made the choices they made. Gradually you feel a new understanding and compassion for them.

"What understanding does this give you?" The Angel asks you and you tell her. "Now you can go back to being you and you feel your heart energy expanding with compassion and love for them. Send them light...send them love. "

Then that scene fades and you are travelling through the night sky with the Angel.

"Now it is time to return to the Garden." She tells you.

Before you can wonder how you will get there you find yourself near the bench in the garden.

"I hope you have some insight from these adventures." The Angel says.

"Yes. Thank you." You tell her.

"Is there anything you have learned?"

"I've learned not to judge people so quickly before tying to understand them and there are some things I will never know about why certain people act as they do. I can still accept them as they are."

"Bless you child." The Angel says. "Life is a series of choices on a moment to moment basis and every choice we have from the thoughts we think to the words we say to the actions we take creates an energy. If we chose more loving, more compassionate actions then they create an energy of a higher vibration that can lift us among the mundane realms of right and wrong on the personality level and to the broader perspective of our souls journey and our life mission."

She puts her hand together and bows slightly as a mark of respect and you do the same. Then she is gone.

At your feet you find a scrap of paper with the affirmation on it.

Affirmation:

I accept good into my life. I allow others to accept good into theirs.

Love
The Angel of Love

Sitting in the Garden of Contemplation you look up to find a glorious Angel by the fountain. She is so bright you can hardly look at her and yet you feast your eyes in wonder at the wonderful white and gold and pink light she emanates.

She says your name and then says "I am the Angel of Love."

Very lovingly she holds out her hand and you take it. She pulls you closer and embraces you and you feel very safe and warm. Suddenly you experience a feeling of love that radiates to you and around you. You also realise that you are radiating love as well as remembering all the times that you have been loving and the people and things that you have loved. In this moment you gain a new insight into those that were not been able to love you back or even who hurt you. You can understand from a higher point of view that they had problems expressing love. Then you realise the Angel is speaking to you.

"All being yearn to love and be loved. Yet learned fears and insecurities can block that expression. Remember, if you are in a difficult communication or conversation with someone silently tell them you love them over and over and feel that love energy flowing from your heart to the person - you will see them respond. Keep silently saying "I love you" to them and you'll notice them open up. The communication will be easier and deeper and they won't know why. Look past their words, past their explanations to what they are really trying to express. Everyone wants to be accepted. Everyone wants to give and receive love. By accepting and loving others you are also accepting and loving yourself."

You are still thinking about her words when she releases you and speaks again.

"There are different levels of love...just as there are different levels of anger or any other emotion. Being "in love" is a deep, total appreciation and pure unconditional acceptance. People often wait to 'find someone perfect ' before they allow themselves to feel that but if you send love to anything and anyone in the universe it will open up your heart chakra and love will teach you its mysteries. When you deeply appreciate someone or something you feel a great deal of love. That love connects you with everything else in the universe and then there is simply the realization of the oneness."

"Through the eyes of love we can appreciate everyone and everything in the universe. Come there are some people I want you to see."

Saying this she lifts you up into the air and above the garden. It is night. The earth is asleep in it's dream world. You travel for many miles until you find that you are both at the edge of the world - on the brink of eternity. A thousand stars shine beneath you and overhead.

She points to a light in the distance and you stare at it. What you think at first is a sphere of gold light slowly reveals itself to be a couple. Hovering, wrapped in a glow of light with a sprinkle of stars two Angels, a man and a woman circle each other encased in the lovely light and energy of love. They are semi transparent and you can tell they are spirits and from their wings you can tell they are angels. By thought transference the Angel of Love speaks to you.

"These two souls have known and loved each other for hundreds of years in different forms." The Angel tells you. "They incarnated into the earth many times and always their spirits recognized each other and longed to be together. Theirs is a spiritual love as they see the loving spirit in each other. Now they can be together here in the Angelic realm of the spirit world."

Then she continues.

"They see the divine in each other. That can be seen when you love look beyond the surface to the inner beauty." She tells you. "Now I will show you the connectedness of all life." She tells you. "All is connected by love."

Suddenly you find yourself in a garden that backs onto a river. A cottage stands behind you and you know, somehow that a magical forest surrounds the garden. You are with someone that you love and this opens your heart to the magic all around you.

The night sky is alive with stars and the full moon looks so serene as she glides through the sky showing radiant beams of light and magic onto the sleeping world.

You feel very alive and sensitive to the energy emanating from everything in the forest. You feel the rustle of the leaves as if they were a part of you. As you watch the full moon over the trees you feel and see her pouring her love down to those same trees in undulating waves that whisper their love to the wind. Next you can see clear,

gentle waves of energy emanated from the trees to the wind. The wind brings the same loving energy to the grasses and flowers by the path where you walked and you realize everything is part of this energy. You realise that truly there is so much love to be a part of that we need never feel lonely. We need only to open to the beauty and life all around us.

"All beings express love in just their very existence" the Angel tells you. "That includes plants and rocks."

You know that you will never again think of anything as inanimate or unaware.

Now another person joins you in this garden. This person is someone you have loved who has passed on to the other side. Yet you immediately know that the love between you still exists. They appear radiantly happy and send you the warm energy of their love. In that moment you realise that love knows no boundaries and is not hampered by time or space or death.

"It is time for you to say good bye and to travel on." The Angel tells you and you say good bye to your friends in the garden. You feel safe in the knowledge of the eternity of love.

"Now you can shine. Let your life be a beacon that shines on the world!" The Angel of Love says.

Saying this she lifts you up in the sky again and guides you through the universe to your home planet.

On the earth the cities are sleeping as you both step out into space and start to feel a warmth emanating from deep within. Every step you take seemingly in the air, takes you higher and a light begins to emanate from you - bright, rich, and warm until the beam touches the grass, the trees, the ocean, the cities of the earth. It feels so good to emanate this light, this love, that comes directly from your heart. You are the sun shining your radiance everywhere you can. A gentle force lifts you high into the sky so you can shine down on all below. You shine on ships crossing the ocean, you see children playing in your glow in the schoolyard, on mothers hanging laundry out to dry in the warmth, people hiking in the hills, playing on the beach or just lying on the sand soaking up the energy you are sending. You feel so joyful and grateful that you are able to send this loving energy to them. You feel their gratitude to you. The cycle continues all over the world. You send your love out and everyone sends it back to you. Now you are passing over your town and see your family and friends. With very little effort you shine your love and light down on them. Feel the healing your power can give them and the changes in their lives...then they send their love back to you...you know everyone had the capability to shine as brightly all over the world.

The Angel of Love leads you back to the Garden of Contemplation, kisses you on the forehead and quietly leaves after handing you a prayer or affirmation.

You feel inspired but then you think realistically of your life on earth. You think of your shortcomings and the things you don't like about yourself and your body. Again the Angel reads your mind.

"Love can transform anything - certainly your body. Send love to every cell in your being. You can bring more love into yourself and into your life." She tells you "Come I will show you. See ways you could bring more love into your life. Starting with yourself. List 20 things you love about yourself. Stand in front of the mirror every day and list them looking into your eyes and finish by saying that you see God in yourself (or whatever your feel is comparable). Learn the subtle art of making people feel better about themselves by casually mentioning the strengths you see in them. Try it with people close to you - let them know you believe in them. Think of everything you do for them as an act of love. Think of your job as an act of love to the world. Give thanks for all the love in your life - in fact give thanks for everything in your life and send your love back to the universe. See it travelling around the world in golden particles of light. Imagine only love exists between you and every other living being on this planet... And the law of the universe is whatever you send out will come back to you. Good bye and blessings to you."

Affirmation:

As I give more love out - it is returned to me and the circle continues eternally.

Goodbye

As you sit on the bench in the Garden of Contemplation you are feeling sleepy and rested from all of your adventures with the Angels. You feel comfortable in the garden and are surprised to see two Angels appear. One of them is Hera, the Angel who talked about wisdom and who greeted you in the Angel Palace when you arrived. The other is Astra, the young Angel who led you here from earth. Astra is as bubbly and Hera is as serene as ever and smiles kindly.

"Greetings again." Hera says. "It is now time for you to leave. But I hope that you have enjoyed your stay here."

In no uncertain terms you tell her that you have.

"Did you have the best time? I knew you would!" Astra gushes. "But, well, its time to go now. I've been asked to take you back."

You feel sad to be leaving but in a way it feels right. The thought of your own room and bed is very appealing.

"I hope that you take with you the lessons learned and the adventures in the Land of the Angels." Hera tells you. "Of course you are welcome back at any time and need only to focus on this place to be back with us."

She embraces you gently. "Blessings to you and may light shine on your path."

You thank her and find that you feel very emotional. It has been a beautiful experience being in this land and you know you will miss it.

"Good bye for now." She tells you.

"Good bye." You say as Astra takes your hand and leads you up into the sky for the last time. After waving to Hera who stays where she is by the fountain you turn and watch where Astra is guiding you. You both travel to the outer edges of the atmosphere of the Land of the Angels. Then you travel through the universe with the stars and planets and the Milky Way. In the distance you see the familiar group of planets and while you have revisited earth many times in your adventures and knowing that you are travelling this way for the last time seems sad. Soon, as you travel, you can pick out earth and see yourself travelling towards it. You break through earth's atmosphere into the sky and travel down towards your country, your town, your street, your home and finally in through the window of your room.

"Well, I have to leave you now." Astra tells you. "But please come and visit us again."

"I will." You promise and then thank her. You embrace and her energy feels light and young. With a wave she is gone like a streak of white light out of your window.

Turning to gaze at your room you see that everything is still the same. In fact after looking at the clock you see that time has not moved at all. You decide it must be all part of the magic. Feeling pleasantly drowsy you climb into bed and fall into a deep sleep and in the morning wonder if it wasn't a dream.

At the dawn of a new age let us leave behind out thoughts of separation,
suffering and neglect. Let us walk into a higher vision of a world
of spiritual love, peaceful thoughts, empowering our friends
and family and seeing past their personalities to their higher selves
that are part of the truth that is within everyone.
We will create a world of beauty for ourselves and our children.

May the Angels guide you with love and light upon
every step of your journey.

Each person thinks that their influence is small but we are
all lights of love for each other.

Lightning Source UK Ltd.
Milton Keynes UK
06 October 2010

160834UK00001B/50/P